The Living Waters Series

Spirit Filled Life
The Unseen Force of Divine Power

By Lori Ann Moeszinger

Memoir

When Death Knocked at My Door:
The 5 Moments that Changed My Life

Autobiography

Total Surrender: My Story
and Your Blueprint for a Meaningful Life

Christian Living

Passion for Christ: New Beginnings

The Living Waters Series

Faith On Trial: The Startling Reality of Genuine Belief

Drenched in Faith: The Transformative Act of Water Baptism

Spirit Filled Life: The Unseen Force of Divine Power

The Bible Unbound: Trust, Translation, and Transformation

Prophets and Pulpits: Discerning Truth in the House of God

Beyond the Tithe: The Transformative Power of Generous Faith

Heart of Abundance: The Journey to Radical Giving and Receiving

Heaven's Reach: Drawing the Unbelieving into the Fold

Breaking Silence: The Charge to Uphold the Faith Out Loud

Beyond the Final Breath: The Christian's Voyage into Eternity

Christian Living

In Sacred Conversation: The New Testament Prayer Guide

The Living Waters Series

Spirit Filled Life
The Unseen Force of Divine Power

By

Lori Ann Moeszinger

THE RIDGE

PUBLISHING GROUP

The Ridge Publishing Group
Coeur d'Alene, Idaho, U.S.A.

CREDIT: This book was written with limited assistance of ChatGPT, an AI language model developed by OpenAI. The collaboration provided unique insights and support in crafting content. The book cover was created using Adobe Photoshop, ensuring a visually captivating infographic and design.

Library of Congress Control Number: 2024923939

Spirit Filled Life: The Unseen Force of Divine Power / by Lori Ann Moeszinger

ISBN: 978-1-956905-51-9 (e-book)
ISBN: 978-1-956905-50-2 (softcover)

1. Religion / Christian Living / General. 2. Religion / Christian Living / Spiritual Growth. 3. Religion / Christian Life / Inspirational. 4. Religion / Christian Life / Personal Growth. 5. Religion / Christian Living / Social Issues. I. Title. II. Title Series

First Edition: October 2024

Printed in the United States of America

Contents

Introduction: What Does   ix
It Mean to Be a Real Christian?

1. The Promise of the Spirit: Exploring
   Biblical Prophecies of the Holy Spirit's Coming   1

2. Pentecost Revisited: The Historical
   Account of the Holy Spirit's Descent   18

3. The Gift for Today: Making the Case
   for the Holy Spirit's Present-Day Baptism   34

4. Voices of Eternity: Understanding the
   Purpose and Power of Speaking in Tongues   53

5. Public vs. Private Utterances: Navigating
   the Different Expressions of Tongues   75

6. The Flame Within: Personal
   Testimonies of the Holy Spirit's Baptism   98

7. Signs of Fire: Instances of Divine
   Presence in Scripture and Modern Times   117

8. A Life Transformed: The Tenfold
   Impact of Embracing the Holy Spirit   138

9. Prayerful Whispers: The Intimacy of
   Praying in Tongues and Its Benefits   161

10. Living the Spirit Filled Life: Daily Walking
    in the Power and Guidance of the Holy Spirit   180

Afterword: Where Do We Go from Here?   198

Bibliography: The Living Waters Series   203

About the Author   221

The Living Waters Series invites readers to rediscover the transformative power of faith. These books open the door to a renewed understanding of devotion, exploring the foundational truths of Christianity with fresh insights and heartfelt sincerity. Whether you are at the start of your spiritual journey or seeking to deepen your faith, these books offer guidance, inspiration, and a renewed sense of connection with Christ.

Join Our Community

Dive deeper into your faith and join a community of like-minded believers by connecting with us across multiple platforms:

- **Facebook Page**: Follow us at Guardians of Biblical Truth to stay updated with inspirational content and community discussions.
- **Facebook Group**: Join our closed group, Guardians of Biblical Truth Forum, for more personal interactions, where you can share, discuss, and grow in your understanding of biblical truths.
- **Blog**: Visit our blog at Jesus-Says.com for thoughtful posts, devotionals, and biblical interpretations aimed at nurturing your spiritual growth.
- **Social Media**: Connect with us on X and Instagram @NNSBible and Pinterest @GuardiansOfBiblicalTruth to get daily inspirations and engage with a community that values deep, scriptural truths.

We look forward to connecting with you and growing together in faith!

The Living Waters Series

Spirit Filled Life

The Unseen Force
of Divine Power

Introduction

What Does It Mean to Be a Real Christian?

Welcome to a journey that will take you beyond the boundaries of the visible world, into the realms of the supernatural. "Spirit Filled Life: The Unseen Force of Divine Power" is a captivating exploration into the profound and often mysterious work of the Holy Spirit in the lives of believers.

In the pages that follow, we will embark on a transformative voyage, uncovering the hidden truths, untold stories, and breathtaking encounters that illuminate the path of the Spirit-filled life. Here, the ordinary becomes extraordinary, the mundane is infused with divine purpose, and the natural gives way to the supernatural.

Together, we will delve into the promises and prophecies of the Holy Spirit in the Bible, tracing His presence from the Old Testament to the New. We will witness the historical accounts of His mighty acts and the personal testimonies of those who have encountered His power in our modern era.

But this journey is not merely a historical or theological exploration; it is an invitation to experience the Holy Spirit's presence and power in your own life. As you read, reflect, and engage with the truths presented, you will find yourself drawn into a deeper, more intimate relationship with the unseen force of divine power that is the Holy Spirit.

Prepare to be inspired, challenged, and transformed as we unlock the secrets of the Spirit-filled life. Whether you are a seasoned believer seeking a fresh encounter with the Spirit or a seeker curious about the supernatural dimensions of faith, this book is your guide to a life enriched by the presence of the Holy Spirit.

Open your heart, open your mind, and open this book. The journey begins now.

Unveiling the Spirit Filled Life: Embracing Divine Power and Presence

As we journey through the chapters of "Spirit Filled Life," you will come to understand that the Holy Spirit is not a distant, abstract concept but a living, breathing presence in your everyday existence. He is the unseen force that empowers, guides, and transforms. He is the divine spark that ignites your faith, the gentle whisper that speaks to your soul, and the source of unshakable hope in a world filled with uncertainties.

Throughout this book, you will encounter stories of individuals whose lives have been forever changed by the Holy Spirit's touch. These are not tales of extraordinary saints but accounts of ordinary people like you and me, who discovered that the Spirit's power is accessible to all who seek it.

We will explore the purpose and power of speaking in tongues, the transformative impact of spiritual gifts, and the profound intimacy of praying in tongues. We will witness the undeniable presence of the Holy Spirit in both ancient scripture and modern times, realizing that the supernatural is not a relic of the past but a vibrant reality for today.

But this book is more than just an exploration; it is an invitation. An invitation to a deeper relationship with the Holy Spirit, an invitation to embrace the unseen force of divine power that is available to you here and now. It is an invitation to embark on your own journey of discovery, to open your heart to the extraordinary possibilities that come with a Spirit-filled life.

So, as we begin this adventure together, I encourage you to approach each page with anticipation and an open heart. Allow the Spirit to guide your thoughts, to ignite your faith, and to awaken your spirit to the wondrous reality of a life filled with the unseen force of divine power.

Let's set forth on this transformative voyage, for the Spirit-filled life awaits, and its mysteries are ready to be unveiled.

The Living Waters Series: An Ongoing Expedition

As we set forth on this sacred journey, it's essential to acknowledge that this is not a finite exploration contained within the pages of a single book. Instead, it's a perpetual quest, an ongoing expedition into the profound depths of faith and spirituality. The Living Waters Series is an ever-flowing river, winding its way through the landscape of our souls, nourishing our spirits, and guiding us to new revelations with every bend in the stream.

In "Spirit Filled Life: The Unseen Force of Divine Power," it will lead us even further into the mysteries of faith, as we delve into the transformative work of the Holy Spirit. It is an invitation to explore the unseen, the ethereal, and the transcendent—a chance to experience the divine force that propels our faith journey forward. But let us remember that this exploration is just one tributary of a much larger river—an exploration that will continue to unfold in future books of the series.

For example, our next destination, "The Bible Unbound: Trust, Translation, and Transformation," will lead us even further into the mysteries of faith, as we delve into the authenticity of Bible translations, unravel prophecy, and deepen your daily faith. Moeszinger offers a clear, engaging guide to understanding the Bible's eternal relevance.

Continuing your journey to a more profound spiritual life, letting God's Word reshape your understanding and purpose.

And beyond that lies a horizon filled with more revelations, deeper understandings, and the boundless grace of God. The Living Waters Series is a testament to our unquenchable thirst for spiritual growth, our unending search for truth, and our unwavering faith in the living God.

So, as we venture into the pages of "Spirit Filled Life," remember that this is not merely a book; it is a tributary of an endless river, a thread in the tapestry of our spiritual expedition. With each book, we draw nearer to the source of living water, and with each page, we drink deeply from the wellsprings of faith.

May your heart be a vessel for these living waters, your soul a canvas for divine revelation, and your spirit a beacon for others seeking to navigate the currents of faith. The journey has begun, dear reader, and it is an adventure like no other—one that beckons you to be drenched in the transformative power of faith's enduring flow.

Invitation

After reading this far, I thank you. With that said, I never start a book without giving an opportunity for people to get right with God. It is really inescapable, the fact that the Bible does teach eternity—once we are born, we live forever. There really is a heaven. There really is a hell. And the Bible tells us that we are going to spend eternity in one of these two places. The choice is ours. God has already made His choice. God loves us. He sent His only Son, Jesus Christ, to die on a cross for the forgiveness of our sins.

> "For God so loved the world, that He gave His only begotten Son, Jesus Christ, that whosoever believes in Him should not perish (cease to exist) but have everlasting life" (John 3:16).

Because God is holy, we need to be holy through Jesus Christ; He will never change, He is immutable, unchangeable. He is in the total state of sinless perfection in everything that He does. But you and I are not holy. By nature, we are sinful and selfish. And because we are sinful and selfish, we are separated from a holy God. But God told us, we were created in His image, and it is His desire to redeem us to right relationship with Him. Therefore, Jesus is the bridge between the holiness of God and the unholiness of humanity. And the Bible also tells us that the only way to break the curse of sin and to find right relationship with God is through Jesus Christ.

> "Jesus says unto him, I am the way, the truth, and the life: no man comes unto the Father, but by Me" (John 14:6).

The Gospel

The word "gospel" in the Greek original text means "good news of the kingdom of God." In Christianity, the term "good news" refers to the story of Jesus Christ's birth, ministry, death, and resurrection. Jesus Christ, the Son of God, died for our sins and rose again, eternally triumphant over His enemies—so that there is now no condemnation for those who believe but only everlasting joy. Wherefore the fullness of the gospel is in God Himself—enjoyed by His redeemed people.

Through the death, the ministry, the burial, and the resurrection of Jesus Christ, you and I not only have power over sin, but we have power over sickness, disease, and infirmity—yesterday, today, and forever. The same seven ways Jesus healed in the New Testament are still available to every believer today. Jesus Christ is still the great physician, and no weapon formed against His children shall prosper in the name of the Lord Jesus Christ.

> "But He was wounded for our transgressions (sins), He was bruised for our iniquities (immoral behavior): the chastisement (punishment) of our peace was upon Him; and with His stripes (the marks on His back from His beating) we are healed" (Isaiah 53:5).

> "Who His own self bore our sins in His own body on the tree (cross), that we being dead to sins, should live unto righteousness: by whose stripes you are healed" (1 Peter 2:24).

Making Peace with God

How do you make peace with God?

You have to do two things:

First, you must believe in the gospel—the teaching and revelation of Christ. The gospel, just as the Scripture says: (1) Jesus Christ, God the Father's only Son, lived on this Earth, (2) died on a cross for the forgiveness of our sins, (3) was buried, (4) was raised from the dead on the third day, (5) stayed on this planet for 40 days before ascending to heaven, (6) promised to return, and (7) we are saved by faith alone in Christ alone—this is called the doctrine of salvation.

Second, you must receive Christ by doing three things: (1) Recognize and admit your sins. The Bible says, "For all have sinned, and come short of the glory of God" (Romans 3:23). (2) Repent of your sins. Jesus said, "No, I tell you; but unless you repent, you will all likewise perish (die)" (Luke 13:3). Repentance means you recognize your sins; you admit your life is headed in the wrong direction, and now you must be willing to turn your back on sin and turn your heart to Christ. (3) Receive Jesus Christ as your personal Lord and Savior. Commit your heart to Him by faith—in childlike faith; showing the good qualities that children have, such as trusting people, being honest and enthusiastic, expressing a childlike innocence or quality.

> "The Lord is not slack concerning His promise, as some men count slackness; but is longsuffering toward us, not willing that any should perish, but that all should come to repentance" (2 Peter 3:9).

That word "men" in the Greek is generic; it means "men and women." Therefore, if you have never recognized and repented of your sins (changed your carnal ways). If you've never had a relationship with God. Or perhaps, you are backslidden or away from God or you've wandered. The Bible says, "I will heal your backsliding, I will love them freely: for My anger is turned away from him" (Hosea 14:4). You can come home to your heavenly Father today, and He will love you, and forgive you, and cleanse you, and strengthen you to be what He's called you to be.

It isn't by accident that you are reading this book. I believe the Lord by His leading and His mercy brought us together. And so, I want to ask you to pray the prayer of salvation—also called the prayer of faith and sometimes called the sinner's prayer—to make peace with God. Just, with a sincere heart, pray the prayer of salvation out loud in childlike faith and make a commitment right now.

Why out loud? Because Christ did everything publicly.

"For whosoever shall be ashamed of Me and of My words, of him shall the Son of Man be ashamed, when He comes in the glory of His Father with His holy angels" (Luke 9:26; also in Mark 8:38).

And after you've done that, go to our Publisher Website at https://www.RidgePublishingGroup.com, and click on "Subscribe" to receive our monthly **Guardians of Biblical Truth New Beginnings Newsletter** sent directly to your inbox. Also, on our website, you will find the prequel to this book, Passion for Christ: New Beginnings, available for free in PDF format when you subscribe. The e-book and print book versions are both available for purchase at Amazon.com and other retailers. Then, follow us on our Amazon Author Central page and learn more about next steps in your walk with God as we upload more Bible-based books. Why? Because this isn't the end of what God's going to do in your life, just the beginning.

> "Go therefore and make disciples of all nations, baptizing them in the name of the Father and of the Son and of the Holy Spirit, teaching them to observe all that I have commanded you. And behold, I am with you always, to the end of the age" (Matthew 28:19-20).

With a sincere heart, just pray this, out loud:

"Heavenly Father, today as I was reading the Bible, you were speaking to me. I want to be right with God. I recognize my sins and I ask for forgiveness. I believe Jesus Christ is your Son. I believe that He died on the cross as payment for sin and rose again as the hope of the world. And I recognize that Jesus is the only salvation and the only Savior available.

In childlike faith, I trust in the Lord Jesus from this day forward. I repent of my sins, and I trust in the blood that was shed on the cross for the forgiveness of my sins. Cleanse me; my mind, my body, and my spirit.

Come into my heart. And I vow this day, I will live for you all the days of my life. Guide my life and help me to do your will. Fill me with the Holy Spirit and give me the power to be what you want me to be. Be my Lord and Savior.

According to the Bible which cannot lie, all who call upon the name of the Lord, shall be saved. Today, I'm saved. I'm forgiven. I'm delivered. I'm healed. The curse of sin and sickness and lack in my life are now broken. And I have become the righteousness of God through Jesus Christ. And I'll never be the same. I pray this in Jesus Christ's precious name. Amen."

The Bible said either your Father is God, or your father is the devil. And the Bible said that the power of sin and Satan comes to steal, and to kill, and to destroy. But Jesus said:

"The thief comes not, but for to steal, and to kill, and to destroy; I come that they might have life, and that they might have it more abundantly" (John 10:10).

Jesus is the master of life. And if you want to walk in the life of forgiveness and have that relationship with God the Father, you can begin that today. All you have to do is pray the prayer of salvation to make peace with God—in doing so, you become a born again Christian.

"Therefore if any man be in Christ, he is a new creature: old things are passed away; behold, all things become new" (2 Corinthians 5:17).

"Total Surrender: My Story and Your Blueprint for a Meaningful Life" is not just an autobiography about my call with God. It is a clarion call (a call to something that is hard to ignore). It is a wakeup call to all of humanity to choose God before it's too late; and get prepared for the second coming of Jesus Christ, our Lord and Savior—time is near, He is knocking at the door:

"Behold, I stand at the door and knock. If anyone hears My voice and opens the door, I will come in to him and eat with him, and he with Me" (Revelation 3:20).

When you know God and understand the wisdom of the Bible, it will change you! This is our calling—our true purpose in life. Let the Lord into your life; He has a plan . . . when you do that, amazing things start to happen: You'll become passionate about God. You'll begin to crave to think and speak in line with Jesus' ways. You'll start to see yourself the way Christ sees you. You'll habitually tune into the Holy Spirit, who lives within those in Christ, to check for a sense of peace in your choices. And then miracles begin to happen . . .

The Promise of the Spirit: Exploring Biblical Prophecies of the Holy Spirit's Coming

"But the Helper, the Holy Spirit, whom the Father will send in my name, He will teach you all things and bring to your remembrance all that I have said to you." — JOHN 14:26 ESV

W elcome to Chapter 1 of "Spirit Filled Life: The Unseen Force of Divine Power." As we open the pages of this captivating journey, we step into a world where ancient prophecies, divine promises, and the timeless presence of the Holy Spirit converge. Picture yourself at the crossroads of history, where prophets of old foresaw the coming of a force beyond human comprehension—a force that would change the course of humanity forever.

In this chapter, we embark on an expedition through the sacred scriptures, where the ink of prophecy met the parchment of revelation. We'll explore the prophetic foretelling of the Holy Spirit, as envisioned by voices from centuries past-voices like Joel, Isaiah, and Ezekiel. These prophets stood as beacons of hope, declaring that God would pour out His Spirit upon all flesh, transcending boundaries of age, gender, and time.

But our journey doesn't stop there. We'll traverse the sands of time to witness the Holy Spirit's intimate involvement in the life and ministry of Jesus Christ. From the moment the Spirit descended like a dove at His baptism to His reliance on the Spirit's guidance throughout His earthly journey, we'll unveil a divine partnership that resonates with profound significance.

And as we delve deeper into the early Christian community, we'll discover how the Holy Spirit's arrival ignited a revolution—a spiritual awakening that empowered and transformed believers. The Comforter, Teacher, and Empowerer became their constant companion, and their lives were forever changed.

This chapter is a prologue to a remarkable narrative—the story of the Spirit-filled life. It's a tale of divine promises fulfilled, of ancient prophecies brought to life, and of an unseen force that continues to shape the destiny of believers today. So, dear reader, fasten your seatbelt and prepare to embark on a journey that will take you to the very heart of the Spirit's power and presence. The adventure begins here.

The Prophetic Foretelling of the Holy Spirit

Chapter 1 sets the stage for our journey into the depths of the Spirit-filled life by delving into the prophetic foretelling of the Holy Spirit. As we embark on this exploration, picture yourself transported to ancient times, where prophets were the messengers of divine hope and promise.

Let's begin with the book of Joel, a prophet whose words resonated with urgency and hope in the midst of adversity. In Joel 2:28-29, he proclaimed, "And afterward, I will pour out my Spirit on all people. Your sons and daughters will prophesy, your old men will dream dreams, your young men will see visions. Even on my servants, both men and women, 1 will pour out my Spirit in those days." Joel's vision of the Holy Spirit's outpouring was like a beacon of light piercing through the darkness of uncertainty. It transcended societal boundaries, offering the promise of divine inspiration and guidance to people of all ages and backgrounds.

Now, turn your attention to the words of the prophet Isaiah. In Isaiah 32:15, he foretells, "till the Spirit is poured on us from on high, and the desert becomes a fertile field, and the fertile field seems like a forest." These words were spoken during a time when Israel faced political turmoil and spiritual drought. Isaiah's prophecy paints a vivid picture of the transformative power of the Holy Spirit, akin to rain quenching the thirst of a barren land, bringing forth abundant growth and life.

Ezekiel, a prophet during the Babylonian exile, offers yet another perspective in Ezekiel 36:26-27: "I will give you a new heart and put a new spirit in you; l will remove from you your heart of stone and give you a heart of flesh. And I will put my Spirit in you and move you to follow my decrees and be careful to keep my laws." In a time of spiritual desolation and captivity, Ezekiel's prophecy speaks of radical inner renewal, where the Holy Spirit not only dwells among God's people but within them, transforming their very nature.

To fully grasp the significance of these prophecies, we must journey back to the historical and cultural contexts of their utterance. These were epochs marked by adversity, exile, and longing for divine intervention. The prophecies of the Holy Spirit's coming were like lifelines, assuring the people that God's presence would not be confined to the past but would be an ever-flowing river of spiritual life.

=====

The Knight and the Promise: A Story
of the Spirit's Power

In a small town, tucked away from the bright lights, lived Fiona, a 35-year-old woman with an indomitable spirit but a burdened heart. Life for Fiona had always been about perseverance. She wore her favorite silver bracelet every day, a reminder of her late mother's love and strength, but it was often overshadowed by her fears and anxieties. As a single mother with two young children, Fiona felt the weight of every worry—how to protect her family, keep them afloat, and somehow find the peace and fulfillment she longed for.

Fiona's days were filled with routine tasks and constant challenges. By night, she lay awake, heart pounding with worry, feeling as though her dreams and strength had dried up, much like the land after a long drought. She remembered her faith, her desire to trust God, but there were moments she felt disconnected, as if some essential part of her spirit was missing.

Then, there was the moment. One evening, after putting her children to bed, Fiona sat in the quiet of her small living room. She was exhausted, yet something deep within nudged her, an almost silent whisper. She reached for an old Bible, flipping through the pages, and her eyes fell on the verse in Joel, "And afterward, I will pour out my Spirit on all people." Something stirred inside her. Could this be for her? She closed her eyes and prayed, with a heart half-believing and half-doubting, asking God for strength, for peace, for something that could quench the dryness in her soul.

In that moment, Fiona felt something she hadn't expected—a warm, gentle presence that was both comforting and invigorating. It was as if a hand had reached into her heart, unlocking hope, strength, and a peace she hadn't known before. Tears streamed down her face as she realized this was the Spirit she'd read about, the one who promised to pour out life and transform even the driest of lands into fertile ground.

Fiona's life began to change. Each morning she felt renewed, not because her circumstances had magically shifted, but because she knew she wasn't alone. She felt stronger, more resilient, and her heart, once weighed down by fear, now beat with hope and purpose. The Spirit was with her, guiding her, renewing her strength as she faced each day with a newfound courage.

For Fiona, the Holy Spirit wasn't a distant force or an abstract concept. He was her strength, her guide, her friend. He turned her midnight worries into quiet moments of assurance, her ordinary days into opportunities for growth. She discovered that the Holy Spirit wasn't just for the saints of old but was available to her, to anyone willing to open their heart and ask.

Fiona's story is more than one woman's journey—it's a promise. The Spirit that transformed her life is available to each of us, ready to quench our thirst, empower us, and help us rise. Like Fiona, we're invited to experience a power that reaches beyond our own, a life filled with purpose, strength, and a peace that speaks even in the silence. This journey is not hers alone but is one for all who are willing to receive the Spirit's transforming presence.

―――――――

The Holy Spirit in the Life of Jesus

In Chapter 1, we continue our captivating journey into the world of the Holy Spirit by focusing on the profound presence of the Spirit in the life and ministry of Jesus Christ. Imagine yourself at the banks of the Jordan River, witnessing a momentous event that marks the beginning of a divine partnership like no other.

One of the most iconic instances of the Holy Spirit's presence in the life of Jesus is His baptism. In the Gospel of Matthew 3:16-17, we read, "As soon as Jesus was baptized, he went up out of the water. At that moment heaven was opened, and he saw the Spirit of God descending like a dove and alighting on him. And a voice from heaven said, This is my Son, whom I love; with him I am well pleased." This breathtaking scene marks the inauguration of Jesus' earthly ministry, with the Holy Spirit descending upon Him like a dove, affirming His divine identity and anointing Him for the task ahead.

As we follow Jesus through His ministry, we witness the profound reliance He placed on the guidance and power of the

Holy Spirit. In Luke 4:1, we find Him led by the Spirit into the wilderness, where He faced and triumphed over temptation. The Spirit served as His constant companion, guiding Him in word and deed.

Moreover, the miracles Jesus performed were often attributed to the power of the Holy Spirit. In Matthew 12:28, Jesus declared, "But if it is by the Spirit of God that I drive out demons, then the kingdom of God has come upon you." This statement underscores the role of the Holy Spirit as the unseen force behind Jesus' extraordinary works, bridging the gap between Old Testament prophecies and their fulfillment in the New Testament.

The continuity of the Holy Spirit's work becomes evident as we journey from the prophetic words of the Old Testament to the living, breathing ministry of Jesus in the New Testament. The Spirit's presence and influence are not confined to a bygone era but flow seamlessly into the life of Christ, fulfilling the promises made by the prophets of old.

By exploring how the Holy Spirit was intricately woven into the very fabric of Jesus' existence and ministry, we gain a deeper understanding of the divine partnership that underpins the Spirit-filled life. This partnership, rooted in Scripture and illuminated by the life of Jesus, serves as an enduring source of inspiration and empowerment for all who seek to follow in His footsteps. In the chapters ahead, we'll delve even deeper into this remarkable journey of faith.

———

The Carpenter and the Dove: A Story of Divine Partnership

In the bustling village of Nazareth lived a young man named Amos. A skilled carpenter in his mid-30s, Amos was known for his craftsmanship and integrity, yet he struggled with an unfulfilled longing—a desire to make a deeper impact in his community. Amos had heard the stories of prophets and miracles but never experienced anything beyond the routine. Life felt predictable, his faith routine. Yet, a spark lingered within him, a hope that one day, God would reveal something extraordinary in his life.

Amos's daily prayer was simple but heartfelt: "Lord, use me for Your purpose. Show me a sign that You're with me." His heart ached for something more substantial than his hands could build—a legacy that would speak to people's souls. Each night, though, he lay awake, wondering if God even heard his prayers.

One day, Amos found himself by the Jordan River, where word had spread that a preacher named John was baptizing people and speaking of the Messiah. Amos felt a pull to witness this for himself, so he joined the crowd. Then, he saw a man step into the water, a man unlike any other. As John baptized this man, the skies opened, and something breathtaking happened. The Spirit of God descended like a dove, resting upon him, and a voice echoed, "This is my Son, whom I love; with him, I am well pleased."

In that moment, Amos felt his own heart stir. This man was Jesus, and Amos sensed he was witnessing the beginning of a divine partnership between Jesus and the Spirit. Amos watched as Jesus was led by the Spirit into ministry, healing the sick, feeding the hungry, and teaching with an authority that only comes from God. Every miracle Jesus performed, every word of hope He spoke, seemed infused with a power far beyond human ability.

One night, as Amos pondered all he had witnessed, he realized that Jesus didn't work alone—His strength and wisdom came from the Holy Spirit. Amos's heart swelled with an understanding that the Spirit could guide, empower, and transform anyone who sought God's purpose. It wasn't just Jesus who was filled with the Spirit; that same divine presence was available to Amos as well.

From that day on, Amos invited the Spirit into his own life, trusting that his everyday work could carry eternal impact. No longer just a carpenter, Amos found new meaning in his craft. As he worked, he prayed for guidance and listened for the Spirit's gentle nudges, finding ways to help others, share wisdom, and bring hope to his neighbors.

Amos's journey reminds us that the Spirit who empowered Jesus is with us too, guiding our actions, emboldening our faith, and turning ordinary lives into extraordinary testimonies. Just as Jesus relied on the Spirit for strength and guidance, so can we, finding in Him the divine partner who brings purpose, strength, and fulfillment beyond what we could ever achieve alone.

―――――――

The Implications of the Holy Spirit's Coming

In Chapter 1, we embark on a thrilling exploration of the implications of the Holy Spirit's coming, uncovering the profound impact it had on the early Christian community and its enduring relevance for believers today. Imagine yourself in the midst of the first-century Christian gatherings, where the presence of the Holy Spirit was palpable, and its transformative power undeniable.

The outpouring of the Holy Spirit on the day of Pentecost, as described in Acts 2:1-4, was a pivotal moment in the early Christian community: "When the day of Pentecost came, they were all together in one place. Suddenly a sound like the blowing of a violent wind came from heaven and filled the whole house where they were sitting. They saw what seemed to be tongues of fire that separated and came to rest on each of them. All of them were filled with the Holy Spirit and began to speak in other tongues as the Spirit enabled them." This supernatural event not only fulfilled the prophecies of old but also ushered in a new era, empowering the disciples and early Christians to boldly proclaim the gospel message.

The Holy Spirit assumed multifaceted roles in the lives of these believers, serving as their Comforter, as promised by Jesus in John 14:16: "And I will ask the Father, and he will give you another advocate to help you and be with you forever." In times of adversity and persecution, the Spirit provided solace, strengthening their faith and resolve.

Furthermore, the Holy Spirit functioned as their Teacher, illuminating the Scriptures and guiding them in truth, fulfilling Jesus' words in John 14:26: "But the Advocate, the Holy Spirit, whom the Father will send in my name, will teach you all things and will remind you of everything I have said to you." This divine guidance ensured the accuracy of their teachings and the preservation of the gospel message.

The Spirit also served as their Empowerer, equipping them with spiritual gifts and enabling them to perform signs and wonders. In Acts 1:8, Jesus foretold this empowerment: "But you will receive power when the Holy Spirit comes on you; and you will be my witnesses in Jerusalem, and in all Judea and Samaria, and to the ends of the earth." The early Christians indeed became powerful witnesses, spreading the message of Christ's salvation far and wide.

The implications of the Holy Spirit's coming were far-reaching, and they continue to reverberate in the lives of believers today. The Comforter, Teacher, and Empowerer who dwelled among the early Christians remains with us, offering solace in times of need, illuminating the Scriptures, and empowering us for our unique callings. As we journey through the chapters ahead, we'll delve deeper into the manifold roles of the Holy Spirit and uncover the rich tapestry of the Spirit-filled life that awaits those who embrace His presence.

The Teacher, The Comforter, and the Strength Within: A Modern Story of the Holy Spirit

In the bustling city of Chicago, Andrew—a teacher in his early forties—was facing one of the toughest seasons of his life. Known for his kindness, Andrew had always found joy in connecting with his students, helping them navigate their own struggles with understanding and empathy. But beneath his warm demeanor, Andrew was now battling grief, and it was a battle he was quietly losing.

The sudden passing of his father had left him shaken. Nights were restless, filled with an aching loneliness, and mornings felt heavier each day. Andrew's once-bright classroom felt shadowed, his energy dimmed by questions he couldn't answer and a pain he couldn't shake. Each day seemed harder than the last, and he wondered how he could continue to pour into his students when he felt so utterly drained himself.

One evening, as Andrew sat alone in his quiet apartment, he opened a small Bible that had belonged to his father. As he read the words, "But the Advocate, the Holy Spirit, whom the Father will send in my name, will teach you all things and will remind you of everything I have said to you" (John 14:26), he felt something stir within him—a glimmer of hope that perhaps he didn't have to walk through this alone.

That night, Andrew prayed a simple prayer: "Holy Spirit, help me find my way through this. I can't carry this on my own."

The following day, as he went through his lessons, Andrew felt an unexpected sense of peace, a comfort that made his burden feel lighter. A few days later, when a student confided in him about a personal struggle, Andrew's words came naturally, filled with empathy and encouragement. He realized that, without knowing it, he was sharing with this student the very comfort he was now beginning to feel himself. He wasn't just teaching facts or figures—he was teaching hope.

In the weeks that followed, Andrew began to notice a shift. The comfort and guidance he had experienced became a steady presence. And beyond just feeling a sense of peace, he felt empowered to reach his students in deeper, more meaningful ways. When he found himself lost for words, the Holy Spirit seemed to provide them. When he needed strength, he felt it from within, a strength that reminded him he was not alone.

In time, Andrew discovered that his role as a teacher had taken on a new depth. He wasn't merely educating young minds—he was inspiring them, encouraging them to see beyond their limitations, much like the Spirit had guided him through his own grief.

Andrew's story is a testament to the Holy Spirit's multifaceted role. As a Comforter, the Spirit gave him peace during his darkest hours. As a Teacher, He provided words of wisdom and encouragement when Andrew was unsure. And as an Empowerer, He infused Andrew with the strength to uplift his students. Andrew realized that just as the Spirit had transformed the early disciples, He was present to transform him too, guiding him through loss and empowering him to bring light to others.

In his classroom, Andrew still honors his father's memory, sharing stories that reflect the love and strength he gained. The Holy Spirit became his companion in this journey, reminding him that the same power that guided the early Christians is alive and active today—available to all who seek comfort, wisdom, and strength for the road ahead.

———

Conclusion

As we draw the curtain on Chapter 1, we've embarked on a voyage through the ages—a journey that has carried us from the hallowed words of ancient prophets to the life and ministry of Jesus Christ, and finally to the transformative impact of the Holy Spirit on the early Christian community. It's a narrative woven with threads of prophecy, promise, and divine presence—a story that continues to unfold in the hearts of believers today.

We've witnessed the fulfillment of prophecies etched into the tapestry of human history, where Joel, Isaiah, and Ezekiel spoke of a coming force—an outpouring of the Holy Spirit that would transcend the limitations of time and culture. This force, as we've seen, was not just a distant promise but a living reality in the life of Jesus Christ.

The Holy Spirit, like a dove descending from the heavens, affirmed Jesus' divine mission at His baptism. We've traced His footsteps through the wilderness of temptation and His ministry of miracles, recognizing the Spirit as His constant guide and source of power. This partnership between Jesus and the Holy Spirit underscores the continuity of God's divine plan, bridging the ancient prophecies of old with the living reality of the New Testament.

Our journey didn't stop with Jesus but extended into the vibrant early Christian community. We've glimpsed the transformative power of the Comforter, Teacher, and Empowerer—the Holy Spirit—who dwelled among the first believers, shaping them into bold witnesses and empowered servants of God.

As we conclude this chapter, we stand at the threshold of a profound truth—the Spirit-filled life is not confined to history; it's an ever-unfolding adventure for all who seek it. The promise of the Holy Spirit, the presence that empowered Christ and transformed His followers, is a promise extended to each of us. It's an invitation to a life that transcends the ordinary, guided by an unseen force that continues to work wonders in the hearts of those who believe.

So, dear reader, as we step forward into the chapters that lie ahead, remember that the story of the Spirit-filled life is not a relic of the past but a living, breathing reality for those who dare to embrace it. The adventure continues, and the best is yet to come.

Pentecost Revisited: The Historical Account of the Holy Spirit's Descent

"All of them were filled with the Holy Spirit and began to speak in other tongues as the Spirit enabled them." — ACTS 2:4 NIV

Welcome to Chapter 2 of our exploration into the Spirit-filled life—a chapter that transports us back in time to one of the most significant days in Christian history: the Day of Pentecost. In the annals of faith, this day shines as a radiant beacon, guiding us through a tapestry of divine events, profound transformation, and the enduring legacy of Pentecost.

As we embark on this captivating journey, imagine yourself standing amidst the bustling streets of Jerusalem, a city steeped in history and tradition. It's the day of Pentecost, a Jewish festival that draws people from diverse nations and cultures to the heart of this ancient city. But within its walls, in a quiet upper room, a group of disciples gathered in obedience to the promise Jesus had made— a promise of an outpouring of the Holy Spirit.

What ensued was nothing short of miraculous—a sound like a "violent wind" filling the room, "tongues of fire" descending and resting upon each disciple, and the astounding phenomenon of speaking in foreign languages. These were not random occurrences but the visible and audible manifestations of the Holy Spirit's arrival. The ordinary had given way to the extraordinary, and the fulfillment of divine promise had begun.

Yet, Pentecost was not just about spectacle; it was about transformation. In the spotlight was Peter, once timid and fearful, now emboldened by the Holy Spirit. He stood before the bewildered crowd, connecting the dots between the prophecies of old and the miraculous events unfolding. His sermon, fueled by the Spirit, boldly proclaimed the life, death, and resurrection of Jesus Christ, leading to a heart-piercing question from the crowd: "What shall we do?" (Acts 2:37).

Peter's response—repentance and baptism—signified a turning point for those who accepted his message. The birth of the early Christian Church was marked not only by rapid growth but by vibrant communal life, devotion to the apostles' teaching, and a radical spirit of sharing and generosity. Signs and wonders performed by the apostles underscored the presence of the Holy Spirit, leaving everyone in awe.

As we traverse the pages of this chapter, we will witness how this legacy of Pentecost reverberated through the early Church, shaping its identity and mission. But more than that, we will uncover the enduring influence of Pentecost in the lives of believers today—a legacy that reminds us of the transformative power of the Holy Spirit and the boundless possibilities that await those who embrace the Spirit-filled life. So, prepare to be captivated by the echoes of Pentecost's enduring influence as we journey deeper into the heart of faith.

The Day of Pentecost: Unpacking the Events

Chapter 2 beckons us to step into the heart of history, revisiting the awe-inspiring Day of Pentecost as recounted in the book of Acts (Acts 2:1-13). It's a moment where the ordinary transcended into the extraordinary-a day when the promise of the Holy Spirit was fulfilled in dazzling fashion.

Picture the scene: Jerusalem, a city steeped in history, was abuzz with people from various nations who had gathered for the Jewish festival of Pentecost. But within the city, in a quiet upper room, a group of disciples were gathered, waiting in anticipation, just as Jesus had instructed. Suddenly, like a tempestuous wind sweeping through, a sound filled the room-a sound like "a violent wind," as described in Acts 2:2. It was a sound that defied explanation, an audible manifestation of the Spirit's arrival.

Then, a sight both mysterious and wondrous—an appearance of "tongues of fire" that "separated and came to rest on each of them" (Acts 2:3). Imagine the disciples' amazement as they beheld these divine flames, a symbol of the Holy Spirit's presence, igniting their very souls.

But the most astonishing phenomenon was yet to come— suddenly, the disciples began to speak in languages they had never learned, proclaiming "the wonders of God" (Acts 2:11). The diverse crowd of pilgrims from various regions were astonished and bewildered. "Aren't all these who are speaking Galileans?" they wondered. It was a miracle that transcended linguistic boundaries, a testament to the power of the Holy Spirit to bridge the gap between cultures and nations.

The reactions of the people were varied —some were amazed, while others were perplexed, even mocking the disciples, suggesting they had indulged in too much wine. Yet, Peter, filled with the Holy Spirit, stood up to explain. It was a moment of transformation for him, as he boldly proclaimed the fulfillment of prophecy and the significance of this event.

This remarkable Day of Pentecost signified the birth of a new era in the early Christian community. It was the moment when the Holy Spirit descended in power, equipping the disciples to fulfill their mission and proclaim the gospel to the ends of the earth. As we delve deeper into the chapters ahead, we'll see how this pivotal day reverberated through history, shaping the course of Christianity and inspiring believers to this day.

———

The Boldness in the Heart: A Pentecost Story of Transformation

Marissa, a young woman in her early twenties, had always been a little reserved. She worked at a small bookstore in her hometown, loved poetry, and had a quiet devotion to her faith. But despite her love for God, she struggled with a constant feeling of inadequacy. Every time she thought about sharing her faith with others, a wave of insecurity and self-doubt would hit her, leaving her silent. She often wondered how anyone as shy as her could make a difference.

One summer evening, her church hosted a special service dedicated to the story of Pentecost. As the speaker recounted the events of that day, Marissa could almost see it: the mighty wind, the flames resting on each disciple's head, the crowd from every corner of the world drawn in by a mystery they couldn't explain. The speaker described the moment when Peter, once uncertain and afraid, was filled with a sudden, unshakable courage. It was the same Peter who had denied Jesus only weeks before, but now he was transformed— speaking boldly and passionately, unashamed and unafraid. That day, thousands were moved by his words.

Something inside Marissa began to stir. She felt a longing for that same courage, that same unshakeable strength. She knew the Holy Spirit was given to every believer, including her, yet she had never truly felt empowered by it. She bowed her head in a silent prayer, asking God to give her the courage to live out her faith more boldly.

In the weeks following that service, something changed. At work one afternoon, she overheard a conversation between two customers—one confided in the other about facing a difficult time. Normally, Marissa would have kept to herself, but before she knew it, she found herself joining in. Gently, she shared her own experience with faith and how God's love had supported her in times of struggle. To her surprise, the woman's eyes welled up with tears, and she thanked Marissa for her words.

This small moment sparked something new. Slowly, Marissa began sharing her faith with her friends and co-workers, not with force but with quiet strength and sincerity. Her heart no longer felt bound by fear; there was a boldness within her that she had never known before. She realized that the same Holy Spirit who had transformed Peter's life at Pentecost was working within her too.

Marissa's story reflects the essence of Pentecost: a moment when ordinary people were empowered to do extraordinary things through the Holy Spirit. Her fear and shyness didn't just vanish; they were transformed into strength, just as the disciples' uncertainty had turned into unbreakable courage.

The Holy Spirit became her source of confidence, bridging the gap between her doubts and her desire to make a difference.

In every person who longs to live out their faith with confidence, the events of Pentecost hold a timeless truth: the Holy Spirit is not confined to history. Today, He's still the source of courage, boldness, and transformation, helping people like Mia step forward with purpose.

Peter's Sermon: The Spirit's Empowerment in Action

In the heart of Chapter 2, we witness the transformation of Peter, one of the disciples, into a powerful preacher. On that unforgettable Day of Pentecost, his sermon marked a turning point in the early Christian community, showcasing the Spirit's empowerment in action.

Peter, emboldened by the Holy Spirit, stood before the bewildered crowd and began to address them. His words were not the mere ramblings of a Galilean fisherman, but a profound message that resonated with clarity and conviction.

First, he addressed the apparent confusion in the crowd, explaining that the disciples were not drunk, as some had speculated, but were filled with the Holy Spirit. He then delved into the Old Testament prophecies, quoting the prophet Joel: "In the last days, God says, I will pour out my Spirit on all people" (Acts 2:17). Peter connected the dots between these prophecies and the extraordinary events unfolding before their eyes, revealing that this was a fulfillment of divine promise.

But Peter's sermon went beyond just connecting the dots; it pierced the hearts of those who listened. He boldly proclaimed the gospel message, attesting to the life, death, and resurrection of Jesus Christ. With conviction, he declared, "God has made this Jesus, whom you crucified, both Lord and Messiah" (Acts 2:36). This declaration carried a weighty truth—Jesus was not merely a historical figure but the Savior and Lord of all.

The impact of Peter's sermon was seismic. The crowd, cut to the heart by his words, asked, "What shall we do?" (Acts 2:37). Peter's response was clear and unequivocal: "Repent and be baptized, every one of you, in the name of Jesus Christ for the forgiveness of your sins. And you will receive the gift of the Holy Spirit" (Acts 2:38). This call to repentance and baptism signified a transformative step—a turning away from sin and a turning toward the grace and forgiveness offered through Christ.

The Holy Spirit's empowerment of Peter was evident not only in his eloquence but also in the profound impact on the crowd. Acts 2:41 records that "those who accepted his message were baptized, and about three thousand were added to their number that day." This was an astounding response, a testament to the Spirit's power to convict hearts and draw people into the fold of faith.

Peter's sermon on the Day of Pentecost serves as a blueprint for effective evangelism and preaching empowered by the Holy Spirit. It illustrates the transformative impact of the Spirit's presence and guidance in the lives of believers, as they boldly proclaim the gospel message, convicting hearts, and drawing souls to Christ. As we continue our journey through this chapter and beyond, we'll see how this empowerment shaped the early Christian Church and continues to impact believers today.

Peter's Turning Point: A Story of Courage and Transformation

Imagine a man named Leo, in his late 30s, who often sat quietly in church, a place he felt connected yet disconnected all at once. He worked as a teacher, loved helping his students learn, but when it came to sharing his faith with others—even his closest friends—he always felt inadequate. His fear of saying the wrong thing or being misunderstood kept his faith hidden behind a veil of silence.

One Sunday, Leo's pastor shared the story of Peter on the Day of Pentecost. The pastor described Peter not as a man of great public speaking ability but as someone who had just recently denied even knowing Jesus out of fear. Yet here was Peter, transformed by the power of the Holy Spirit, boldly standing before a massive crowd to proclaim the gospel. Leo could hardly imagine the courage it must have taken. But he was struck by the idea that Peter wasn't relying on his own strength or eloquence; he was empowered by something far greater.

That night, Leo lay awake thinking of Peter's transformation and asked God to help him break free from his own fears. He prayed for courage, and though he didn't know how, he believed that, like Peter, he too could be empowered by the Holy Spirit.

Not long after, Leo found himself in a casual conversation with his colleague, Dan. Dan was going through a difficult time and confided his frustration and doubts. Normally, Leo would listen quietly, but that day, he felt a nudge—a sense of clarity and confidence he hadn't known before. Gently, he began to share how his faith helped him find peace even in life's darkest moments. He even mentioned Peter's story, explaining how transformation is possible when we allow God to work through us.

To Leo's surprise, Dan was deeply moved. He thanked Leo for his words and said it gave him hope, something he hadn't felt in a long time.

That small conversation marked a turning point for Leo. The next time he felt a nudge to speak up, he didn't hesitate. His heart was no longer bound by fear, and he realized that he was not alone in these moments—the Holy Spirit was empowering him to share his faith with sincerity and courage, just as Peter had done on that monumental day at Pentecost.

Leo's story reflects the timeless truth of Pentecost: when we are empowered by the Holy Spirit, we find strength beyond our own abilities. Leo's fear gave way to faith, and his quiet personality didn't limit him; instead, it became the perfect vessel for God's gentle yet powerful message. His courage grew, and his relationships deepened as he shared his faith with others.

In each of us, there lies the same potential for transformation. Like Peter, we may feel inadequate or fearful, but the Holy Spirit gives us the courage to step beyond our comfort zones and bring hope to those around us. And just as Peter's words resonated with thousands, so too can our words, empowered by the Spirit, reach those who need them most.

The Birth of the Church: Pentecost's Lasting Legacy

In the wake of the electrifying events on the Day of Pentecost, the birth of the early Christian Church emerged as a defining moment in the history of faith. It was a time marked by rapid growth, unparalleled unity, and the unwavering influence of the Holy Spirit, shaping the identity and mission of the Church in remarkable ways.

Immediately following Peter's powerful sermon, something extraordinary happened. Acts 2:41 tells us, "Those who accepted his message were baptized, and about three thousand were added to their number that day." It was a monumental surge in the Christian community—a testament to the profound impact of the Spirit's empowerment and the compelling message of Christ's salvation.

But the birth of the Church was not merely about numbers; it was about the vibrant communal life of believers. Acts 2:42 paints a vivid picture of their daily activities: "They devoted themselves to the apostles' teaching and to fellowship, to the breaking of bread and to prayer." This was a community marked by devotion to the Word of God, a deep sense of fellowship, and a shared commitment to prayer—a bond strengthened by the Holy Spirit.

One of the most striking aspects of this early Christian community was their radical generosity. Acts 2:44-45 reveals, "All the believers were together and had everything in common. They sold property and possessions to give to anyone who had need." This communal sharing of possessions was a reflection of their deep unity and love for one another, a tangible expression of Christ's teachings and the Holy Spirit's influence.

The ongoing signs and wonders performed by the apostles further solidified the Church's identity and mission. Acts 2:43 states, "Everyone was filled with awe at the many wonders and signs performed by the apostles." These miraculous manifestations, empowered by the Holy Spirit, served as powerful testimonies to the truth of the gospel and the presence of God among them.

Pentecost's lasting legacy was the birth of a Church that transcended mere human organization. It was a Church infused with the life and power of the Holy Spirit—a community characterized by unity, devotion, radical generosity, and a mission to proclaim the gospel to the ends of the earth. As we journey through the chapters ahead, we'll see how this legacy continued to shape the early Church and continues to inspire believers to this day, reminding us of the profound impact of Pentecost's enduring influence.

A New Beginning: The Impact of Pentecost on the Birth of the Church

Imagine Kayla, a young woman in her early twenties who had grown up feeling isolated and searching for a place to truly belong. Though she had attended church occasionally, she often felt disconnected, longing for a deeper sense of community. She moved to a bustling city for a new job, excited but unsure of how to find her place.

One evening, she passed a small community gathering near her neighborhood and noticed people laughing, sharing food, and helping each other with genuine warmth. Intrigued, she decided to join them the next time they met. To her surprise, it wasn't just another social club—it was a group of believers deeply committed to supporting one another, praying together, and growing in their faith.

Kayla felt something different that night. The group explained how their connection and generosity were modeled after the early Christian community born on the Day of Pentecost. They shared how the Holy Spirit empowered the early Church to become a thriving, united family marked by radical generosity, love, and purpose. Each person there had a story of finding belonging and transformation, and Kayla found herself drawn to their words and their sense of shared mission.

It was a pivotal moment for Kayla. As she continued to meet with this group, she experienced a newfound closeness with God and others that she had always longed for. Her life began to change in small but powerful ways: her anxiety softened, her confidence grew, and she started volunteering to help others in need. She even found herself sharing her story with friends and inviting them to experience this community, just as she had been invited.

For Kayla, this community became a modern reflection of the early Church's spirit—a place of unity, selfless giving, and authentic love, all guided by the Holy Spirit's influence. Just as the Holy Spirit had inspired the early believers to come together, support one another, and spread hope to the world, Kayla felt this same calling in her own life.

Her experience is a testament to Pentecost's lasting legacy, showing how the Holy Spirit continues to bring people together in unity and purpose. The same Spirit that empowered Peter and the apostles now empowers believers like Kayla, reminding us that the Church is more than a building—it's a living, breathing community shaped by love and purpose. Through the legacy of Pentecost, the Church continues to be a place where people can find not only faith but a family, and Kayla's story is a beautiful example of that unbreakable bond.

───────

Conclusion

As we bring the curtain down on Chapter 2, we find ourselves standing on sacred ground-the ground where the Day of Pentecost unfolded in all its glorious splendor. We've retraced the footsteps of history, witnessed the astonishing events of that transformative day, and felt the heartbeat of the early Christian Church quicken with the Holy Spirit's indomitable power.

Pentecost, as we've seen, was not a mere historical event but a seismic shift in the spiritual landscape. It was the day when the divine promise of the Holy Spirit became a living reality, setting hearts ablaze and tongues free to proclaim the message of Christ. The details-rushing wind, tongues of fire, and the gift of languages -speak of a supernatural power that defies explanation.

Yet, Pentecost was more than a spectacle; it was a catalyst for change. Peter, once a timid disciple, became a bold preacher, eloquently declaring the gospel message to a captivated crowd. The response—repentance, baptism, and the birth of the early Christian Church—underscored the Spirit's transformative influence.

The communal life of believers, marked by devotion, fellowship, and radical generosity, reflected the unity and love that flowed from the Holy Spirit. Signs and wonders, performed by the apostles, bore witness to the living presence of God among them.

But as we conclude this chapter, we must remember that Pentecost's legacy is not a relic of the past; it's an enduring force that continues to shape the Church and the lives of believers today. The Spirit-filled life, ignited by the events of Pentecost, beckons us to experience the transformative power of the Holy Spirit in our own journey of faith.

So, dear reader, as we move forward into the chapters ahead, let the echoes of Pentecost resonate in your heart. Embrace the legacy of this historic day, for it is a legacy of empowerment, unity, and unwavering devotion—a legacy that invites you to step into the Spirit-filled life, where the extraordinary becomes ordinary and the power of the Holy Spirit knows no bounds. The adventure continues, and the best is yet to come.

CHAPTER THREE

The Gift for Today: Making the Case for the Holy Spirit's Present-Day Baptism

"The promise is for you and your children and for all who are far off—for all whom the Lord our God will call." — ACTS 2:39 NIV

Welcome, dear reader, to Chapter 3, a chapter that invites you to embark on a captivating journey—a journey that traverses the corridors of time, explores the tapestry of faith, and unveils the profound and transformative power of the Holy Spirit's baptism. In this chapter, we step into the heart of the Spirit-filled life, a place where the ordinary becomes extraordinary, the timeless meets the contemporary, and the divine intersects with the human. It is a journey that takes us on a multidimensional exploration, drawing wisdom from the sacred pages of Scripture, connecting with the annals of history, and forging a deep connection with the personal experiences of believers in our time.

As we navigate the landscapes of this chapter, we will delve into the very essence of the Spirit-filled life—a life where the Holy Spirit's baptism is not a relic of the past but a living, breathing reality. Through narratives of faith, empowerment for ministry, and spiritual growth, we will witness the Holy Spirit's ongoing work in the lives of individuals today. These stories are not isolated incidents but integral threads woven into the fabric of the Christian community, testifying to the enduring relevance and life-changing impact of the Holy Spirit's baptism.

So, prepare to be captivated by the unseen force of divine power—the Holy Spirit—whose presence knows no boundaries, whose impact knows no limits, and whose invitation to a transformative journey of faith is extended to you, here and now. Join us as we unravel the mystery, explore the profound significance, and encounter the living reality of the Holy Spirit's baptism—a journey that promises to enrich your faith, empower your ministry, and propel your spiritual growth.

Biblical Foundations of the Holy Spirit's Baptism

In Chapter 3, we embark on a journey to uncover the biblical foundations of the Holy Spirit's baptism—a truth that continues to shape the lives of believers today. Our quest begins with the sacred pages of the New Testament, where we find passages that illuminate the timeless nature of this divine encounter.

One such passage, Acts 8:14-17, tells the story of Philip's ministry in Samaria. He preached the gospel, and as people believed, they were baptized in the name of Jesus Christ. But there was more to come. When the apostles in Jerusalem heard about this, they sent Peter and John to Samaria. What happened next was extraordinary: "They prayed for the new believers to receive the Holy Spirit, for as yet, he had not come upon any of them. They had only been baptized in the name of the Lord Jesus. Then Peter and John laid their hands upon these believers, and they received the Holy Spirit" (Acts 8:15-17).

This passage is a pivotal piece of evidence for the ongoing experience of the Holy Spirit's baptism. It reveals that there is more to the Christian journey than water baptism; there is a subsequent encounter with the Holy Spirit, a divine infusion that empowers believers to walk in the fullness of their faith.

Another compelling passage, Acts 19:1-7, transports us to the city of Ephesus, where Paul encountered a group of disciples who had received John the Baptist's baptism but had not yet experienced the Holy Spirit's baptism. Paul asked them, "Did you receive the Holy Spirit when you believed?" Their response, "No, we have not even heard that there is a Holy Spirit," underscores the importance of understanding this aspect of the Christian journey. Paul then baptized them in the name of the Lord Jesus, laid his hands on them, and the Holy Spirit came upon them. It was a transformative moment that mirrored the events of the early Church.

These passages, among others, provide a solid scriptural foundation for the concept of the Holy Spirit's baptism in contemporary Christian life. They remind us that our faith is not limited to a one-time event but is an ongoing journey of encountering the living God. As we explore this biblical foundation further, we'll uncover the enduring relevance and transformative power of the Holy Spirit's baptism in the lives of believers today.

Our exploration of the biblical foundations for the Holy Spirit's baptism extends beyond Acts to other key passages in the New Testament, reinforcing the concept of this divine encounter as a continuous and essential aspect of the Christian experience.

One such passage can be found in the Gospel of John, where Jesus Himself promises the coming of the Holy Spirit. In John 14:16-17, Jesus says, "And I will ask the Father, and he will give you another Helper, to be with you forever, even the Spirit of truth, whom the world cannot receive because it neither sees him nor knows him. You know him, for he dwells with you and will be in you." These words convey the ongoing presence and indwelling of the Holy Spirit in the lives of believers, a promise that transcends time and culture.

Furthermore, in the book of Acts, we witness the Holy Spirit's baptism as a recurring phenomenon. Beyond the instances in Acts 8 and Acts 19, the early Church continued to experience this transformative encounter. Acts 2, the Day of Pentecost, sets the precedent as believers were filled with the Holy Spirit, an event that transcended a single day and continued to shape their lives and ministry.

As we delve deeper into the pages of the New Testament, we discover a tapestry of passages that affirm the enduring nature of the Holy Spirit's baptism. This biblical foundation serves as a timeless reminder that the Spirit-filled life is not a relic of the past but a living reality for believers today. It's an invitation to embrace the fullness of our faith, empowered by the same Spirit who moved in the early Church, shaping their identity and mission.

So, as we journey through the chapters ahead, let us do so with the assurance that the Holy Spirit's baptism is not a historical artifact but a divine gift for today—a gift that empowers, transforms, and empowers believers to walk in the fullness of their faith.

The Divine Encounter: Embracing the Power
of the Holy Spirit's Baptism

Meet Isaiah, a devoted husband and father in his mid-thirties, whose life seemed complete on the outside, but who felt a gnawing sense of emptiness deep within. Though he had been raised in church, attended faithfully, and was even baptized in water as a teenager, he knew there was something missing—a hunger for a deeper connection with God that he couldn't quite explain. His faith was real, but it lacked the vibrancy and power he had read about in the New Testament.

Isaiah often found himself wondering late at night: Is there more to my walk with God than what I'm experiencing? Despite his involvement in church, he felt as though he was merely going through the motions, yearning for a personal encounter with God that would breathe life into his faith.

One evening, during a mid-week Bible study, a guest speaker introduced the topic of the Holy Spirit's baptism and its impact on the early Christians. As he shared stories from Acts 8 and Acts 19, Isaiah found himself captivated, resonating with the experiences of those early disciples who discovered there was indeed "more." The speaker emphasized that the Holy Spirit's baptism was not just a historical event, but a present-day reality, available to all who sought it.

In that moment, something shifted for Isaiah. The speaker invited anyone who desired this deeper connection with the Holy Spirit to come forward. Without hesitation, Isaiah stepped up, his heart pounding with anticipation. As others began to pray with him, Isaiah felt a presence unlike anything he had ever known—a warmth, a peace, and a boldness filling his spirit. It was as if his heart, long searching, had found its answer. He knew then that the Holy Spirit was real, personal, and powerful, infusing his life with a newfound courage to live out his faith boldly.

From that night forward, Isaiah's life took on a new dimension. He found himself speaking to others about his faith with confidence and joy he hadn't known before. His prayers became deeper, and his connection with God more intimate and tangible. It was no longer just a routine but a living, breathing relationship with the Holy Spirit guiding him.

Isaiah's story is a testament to the life-changing power of the Holy Spirit's baptism, affirming that this divine encounter isn't just for the first-century church but for believers today. His transformation shows us that the Holy Spirit's baptism is a gift that brings vitality, courage, and purpose to our faith. It reminds us that our walk with God is meant to be dynamic and ever-growing—a journey of continual empowerment through the Spirit.

Historical Perspectives and Revival Movements

In our quest to understand the present-day relevance of the Holy Spirit's baptism, we must also journey through history, where we discover a rich tapestry of Christian revival movements that played a pivotal role in emphasizing this ongoing experience. These historical perspectives provide valuable insights into how the Holy Spirit's baptism has shaped the modern Christian landscape.

One notable landmark on our historical journey is the Azusa Street Revival, which unfolded in Los Angeles in the early 20th century. Led by William J. Seymour, this revival is often considered the birthplace of the modern Pentecostal movement. It was characterized by an outpouring of the Holy Spirit, with participants experiencing speaking in tongues, healing, and other manifestations of the Spirit's presence. The Azusa Street Revival served as a powerful reminder that the Holy Spirit's baptism was not a relic of the past but a dynamic force still at work, echoing the promise Jesus made to His disciples in Acts 1:8: "But you will receive power when the Holy Spirit has come upon you, and you will be my witnesses in Jerusalem and in all Judea and Samaria, and to the end of the earth."

Another significant historical milestone is the Charismatic Renewal that swept through various Christian denominations in the mid-20th century. This movement emphasized the experience of the Holy Spirit's baptism and spiritual gifts, drawing from passages like 1 Corinthians 12 and 1 Corinthians 14, which highlight the diverse manifestations of the Spirit. The Charismatic Renewal breathed fresh life into the understanding of the Holy Spirit's role in contemporary Christian life and emphasized the need for believers to eagerly desire spiritual gifts, as outlined in 1 Corinthians 14:1.

These historical occurrences have left an indelible mark on modern views of the Holy Spirit's baptism. They have reminded believers that the Holy Spirit is not a distant figure of the past but a present-day reality. The Spirit's empowering presence, as seen in Acts 2:38-39, where Peter declares, "Repent and be baptized every one of you in the name of Jesus Christ for the forgiveness of your sins, and you will receive the gift of the Holy Spirit. For the promise is for you and for your children and for all who are far off, everyone whom the Lord our God calls to himself," continues to be accessible and transformative.

As we reflect on these historical perspectives and revival movements, we gain a deeper appreciation for the ongoing relevance of the Holy Spirit's baptism. It's a reminder that the Spirit-filled life is not confined to a single era but is a gift for every generation, empowering believers to live out their faith boldly and to be effective witnesses of Christ's love and power in a changing world.

These historical perspectives and revival movements offer us more than a mere glimpse into the past; they provide valuable lessons for the present. They underscore the importance of remaining open to the dynamic work of the Holy Spirit, echoing the exhortation in Ephesians 5:18, which encourages believers to "be filled with the Spirit." This filling, as exemplified in the Azusa Street Revival and the Charismatic Renewal, is not a one-time event but an ongoing experience that empowers believers for effective ministry and personal transformation.

Moreover, these movements have highlighted the unity and diversity within the body of Christ. The Holy Spirit's baptism transcends denominational boundaries and theological differences, uniting believers in their shared desire for a deeper experience of God's presence. Galatians 3:28 reminds us, "There is neither Jew nor Greek, there is neither slave nor free, there is no male and female, for you are all one in Christ Jesus." The Holy Spirit's work knows no discrimination, and His baptism is available to all who seek it with sincere hearts.

In considering these historical perspectives, we gain a broader perspective on the Holy Spirit's role in contemporary Christian life. The legacy of the Azusa Street Revival, the Charismatic Renewal, and similar movements reminds us that the Holy Spirit's baptism is not confined to a single tradition or movement but is a vibrant reality for the entire body of Christ.

As we continue our exploration of the Holy Spirit's baptism, let us draw inspiration from these historical milestones. They encourage us to embrace the fullness of the

Spirit's work, to seek a deeper encounter with God, and to remain open to the transformative power of the Holy Spirit in our lives and in the Church today.

———————

A Legacy of Transformation: Embracing the Power of the Holy Spirit in Every Era

Meet Madeline, a young woman in her late twenties, who grew up in a traditional church where faith was quiet, predictable, and respectful. Though she loved the beauty and order of her upbringing, she often sensed something missing—a dynamic, intimate experience with God that felt real, personal, and powerful. Madeline had heard about believers who spoke of a "Spirit-filled life," but in her context, it seemed distant, something that happened in faraway places or in the stories of others.

One evening, after a conversation with a close friend, Madeline came across a book on the Azusa Street Revival. She read about the remarkable outpouring of the Holy Spirit in a modest warehouse in Los Angeles in 1906, led by a humble pastor, William J. Seymour. People from all walks of life and backgrounds came together to experience God in a way Madeline had never imagined. She learned how attendees spoke in new languages, witnessed miraculous healings, and carried an unshakable sense of joy and unity. For the first time, Madeline saw that the Holy Spirit was not just a theological concept; He was a living, transforming presence who could change lives and empower people in ways beyond human limitations.

But the story that truly captivated Madeline was about the Charismatic Renewal of the mid-20th century. This wasn't just one church or one denomination; the Holy Spirit had swept across the lines of traditional boundaries and denominational divisions. Here were people from diverse backgrounds—Catholics, Lutherans, Methodists—united by a shared experience of the Spirit's power. The stories from the renewal were clear: the Holy Spirit's baptism was not limited to one era or type of believer. It was for everyone, right here and now.

Madeline felt a stirring in her heart—a desire to experience the Holy Spirit in her own life. One Sunday, she attended a service where the pastor spoke about the Holy Spirit's power and invited anyone who wanted a deeper connection with God to pray for the Spirit's filling. With her heart pounding, Madeline went forward, opening herself to the possibility of God's power in a way she had never dared before. As she prayed, she felt a warmth fill her heart, a peace that transcended words, and a joy that seemed to illuminate her from within. Madeline's experience was transformative—she found a courage she'd never known before, a newfound passion for her faith, and an eagerness to share God's love with others.

Madeline's journey reminds us that the legacy of revival movements, like Azusa Street and the Charismatic Renewal, extends beyond the walls of time and place. These historical movements illustrate the enduring relevance of the Holy Spirit's baptism, a gift that transcends boundaries and generations. Just as the Spirit transformed lives a century ago, He is equally available to transform lives today, bringing people into a vibrant relationship with God.

Madeline's story is a powerful reminder that the Holy Spirit's baptism is not a relic of the past; it's an ongoing invitation into a life of faith, boldness, and unity, available to all who seek with sincere hearts.

Contemporary Testimonies and Impact

In the tapestry of our faith, it is essential to weave together the threads of contemporary testimonies-vivid stories of individuals whose lives have been profoundly touched by the Holy Spirit's baptism. These narratives serve as living testaments to the enduring relevance and life-changing power of this divine encounter, drawing us closer to understanding its impact on personal faith, ministry, and spiritual growth.

Meet Florence, a young woman whose life was transformed through the Holy Spirit's baptism. Raised in a Christian family, she had always known about the Holy Spirit but had never fully experienced His presence. Then, during a worship service, as the lyrics of a familiar hymn filled the room, she felt an overwhelming sense of God's love and peace wash over her, like a gentle stream of living water. It was a moment reminiscent of Jesus' promise in John 7:38: "Whoever believes in me, as the Scripture has said, 'Out of his heart will flow rivers of living water.'" For Florence, this experience was a turning point—a deep encounter with the Holy Spirit that rejuvenated her faith and ignited a passion for worship and ministry she had never known before.

Moses's story takes us into the realm of empowerment for ministry. As a pastor, he had often taught about the Holy Spirit's role in the lives of believers but had yet to experience the Spirit's baptism in a profound way himself. One day, while praying for his congregation, he sensed an overwhelming surge of God's presence and power. It was as if Acts 1:8 had come to life in his ministry: "But you will receive power when the Holy Spirit has come upon you, and you will be my witnesses in Jerusalem and in all Judea and Samaria, and to the end of the earth." Moses's preaching and pastoral care were forever transformed, bearing fruit beyond his expectations, as he discovered the Spirit's empowerment to be a reality.

These contemporary testimonies underscore the transformative impact of the Holy Spirit's baptism on personal faith, empowerment for ministry, and spiritual growth. They are not isolated incidents but part of a larger tapestry of stories within the Christian community, reminding us that the Holy Spirit's work is not confined to the pages of Scripture or the annals of history; it is alive and active in the lives of believers today.

As we hear these testimonies, we are reminded of the Apostle Paul's words in 1 Corinthians 2:4-5: "My message and my preaching were not with wise and persuasive words, but with a demonstration of the Spirit's power, so that your faith might not rest on human wisdom, but on God's power." These stories serve as living demonstrations of God's power at work in our midst, inviting us to seek a deeper encounter with the Holy Spirit and to embrace the transformative potential of the Spirit-filled life in our own journeys of faith.

Now, let's meet Lorelei, a woman whose journey exemplifies the impact of the Holy Spirit's baptism on spiritual growth and maturity. Lorelei grew up in a Christian home, attending church regularly and learning about the Holy Spirit from a young age. However, it wasn't until her adult years that she truly encountered the depth of the Spirit's presence. During a season of personal struggle and doubt, Lorelei sought solace in prayer and reflection. One evening, as she poured out her heart to God, she felt an overwhelming sense of His comforting presence, as described in Psalm 34:18: "The Lord is near to the brokenhearted and saves the crushed in spirit." This encounter with the Holy Spirit brought her a newfound sense of spiritual maturity, deepening her understanding of God's love and wisdom. It was a transformative moment that propelled her into a season of spiritual growth and a hunger for God's Word.

These diverse testimonies highlight the enduring relevance and profound impact of the Holy Spirit's baptism in today's

Christian community. They remind us that the Spirit-filled life is not a distant dream but a tangible reality—a journey of faith marked by encounters with the living God.

As we contemplate these contemporary stories, we're invited to embark on our own spiritual journey, seeking the transformative power of the Holy Spirit's baptism. Whether we are like Florence, yearning for a fresh encounter with God's love, Moses, desiring empowerment for ministry, or Lorelei, seeking spiritual growth and maturity, the Holy Spirit stands ready to meet us where we are.

In the chapters ahead, we will continue to explore the depths of the Spirit-filled life, guided by the wisdom of Scripture, the lessons of history, and the powerful testimony of believers today. So, let us embrace these stories as beacons of hope, leading us toward a deeper, more vibrant faith—a faith enriched by the presence and power of the Holy Spirit, a faith that knows no boundaries and encounters no limits.

Encountering the Spirit: A Journey to Deeper Faith and Transformation

Meet Gracie, a 34-year-old teacher, always active in her church and familiar with the stories of the Holy Spirit from the Bible. Yet, despite her commitment, Gracie often felt a gap between the vibrant faith she read about in Scripture and her own experience. She struggled with a quiet but persistent feeling of spiritual dryness—a sense that, while her faith was genuine, it lacked the power and intimacy she longed for. Late one night, sitting alone after another busy day, she felt an ache in her heart and prayed, "God, is there something more?"

One Sunday, Gracie joined a close friend at a worship service where she heard firsthand stories of people touched by the Holy Spirit. She listened intently to a woman named Stella, who shared how an encounter with the Spirit had transformed her life from ordinary to extraordinary. Abigale described a similar longing, but one night, while praying, she had felt a sudden wave of peace and love wash over her, igniting a joy she had never known. Her life was never the same—her faith became vibrant, her prayers confident, and her relationship with God felt real and alive. Listening, Gracie felt a spark of hope. Could the Holy Spirit bring that kind of transformation to her, too?

The following week, Gracie found herself drawn to her church's prayer group, where the leaders offered a prayer for those desiring a closer relationship with the Holy Spirit. She prayed along with them, and then, as she opened her heart fully to God, a warmth filled her chest, a peace that brought tears to her eyes. In that moment, Gracie knew she wasn't alone. She felt as if God was right there with her, answering her deepest questions and meeting her exactly where she was. She found herself praying words of thanks, feeling love and gratitude flow through her as she experienced a closeness she'd never felt before.

From that night, Gracie noticed a marked change in herself. She had a renewed hunger for prayer and a joy that spilled into her daily life. Her interactions with her students became more patient and filled with compassion. Her faith felt unshakable, no longer fueled by obligation but by a genuine connection with God's Spirit. In short, the Holy Spirit's baptism had transformed Gracie's faith from a quiet routine into an active, empowering relationship.

Gracie's story reminds us that the Holy Spirit isn't a distant force or confined to stories of the past. Just as Gracie found, the Spirit is a real, transformative presence available to anyone who seeks. Whether we're yearning for fresh faith, desiring deeper spiritual growth, or simply wondering if God can fill the gap we feel, the Holy Spirit meets us where we are, offering renewal, empowerment, and connection. For Gracie and many others, this isn't just a chapter of faith—it's the life-giving heart of it, an invitation to anyone seeking something more.

Conclusion

As we draw the curtain on Chapter 3, we find ourselves at the intersection of history, faith, and personal encounters with the Divine—an intersection that pulsates with the vitality of the Holy Spirit's baptism. These stories, both ancient and contemporary, have taken us on a captivating journey, unveiling the enduring relevance and life-transforming power of this divine encounter.

We've seen how individuals like Gracie, Moses, and Lorelei have been touched by the Holy Spirit's baptism in profound ways. Their experiences reflect the multi-dimensional impact of the Spirit-filled life: from a deep encounter with God's love, to empowerment for ministry, and spiritual growth beyond measure. Their stories remind us that the Holy Spirit's work is not confined to distant history but is an ever-present reality, an invitation extended to each of us.

As we reflect on these narratives, we find ourselves standing at the threshold of our own journey—a journey into the depths of faith, a journey where the Holy Spirit's baptism is not a mere concept but a vibrant, transformative encounter. It is an invitation to explore the unseen force of divine power, to seek deeper encounters with God, and to embrace a life enriched by the Holy Spirit's presence and empowerment.

The pages ahead hold more discoveries, more revelations, and more opportunities to engage with the living reality of the Spirit-filled life. So, dear reader, let these stories be the wind in your sails as you embark on your own adventure—a journey into the heart of faith, a journey where the Holy Spirit's baptism is not a distant dream but a tangible, life-changing reality. The best is yet to come, and the Spirit's work continues to unfold.

CHAPTER FOUR

Voices of Eternity: Understanding the Purpose and Power of Speaking in Tongues

"For anyone who speaks in a tongue does not speak to people but to God. Indeed, no one understands them; they utter mysteries by the Spirit." — 1 CORINTHIANS 14:2 NIV

Welcome, dear reader, to Chapter 4—an exploration into the captivating world of speaking in tongues. This spiritual phenomenon has been a source of fascination, inspiration, and sometimes perplexity for believers across the ages. It's a topic that stirs the imagination, sparks devotion, and ignites conversations within the Christian community. In this chapter, we embark on a remarkable journey, a voyage that transcends the boundaries of language and plunges us into the depths of the divine.

Speaking in tongues, often referred to as the "language of heaven," continues to be a dynamic and relevant facet of the Spirit-filled life. As we set sail into this intriguing territory, we'll unearth its deep biblical roots, unveil its multifaceted purposes, and lend our ears to the voices of contemporary believers who have encountered its transformative power. Prepare to be immersed in the symphony of voices from eternity, for within the diversity of tongues, we discover not only a captivating mystery but also a profound and profoundly spiritual expression of faith.

Our journey takes us beyond the surface, seeking to comprehend the profound purpose and the potent power that reside within the gift of speaking in tongues. It is an exploration that beckons us to peer into the pages of sacred scripture, to navigate the waters of contemporary testimonies, and to contemplate the eternal significance of this spiritual gift. As we delve deeper into the heart of this topic, we will uncover layers of understanding, each revealing a facet of the intricate tapestry that is the Spirit-filled life.

In the chapters that follow, we'll embark on a quest to understand not just the "how" but also the "why" of speaking in tongues—a journey that promises to enrich our understanding of this enigmatic gift and to illuminate its relevance and impact in the modern Christian experience.

So, prepare to be captivated, inspired, and perhaps even surprised as we venture further into the world of speaking in tongues, for in the midst of its diverse expressions, we find a powerful and deeply spiritual expression of faith that transcends earthly boundaries and connects us with the divine.

The Biblical Basis of Speaking in Tongues

In this chapter, we embark on a fascinating journey to uncover the biblical basis of speaking in tongues, a gift often surrounded by intrigue and curiosity. We start our exploration in the book of Acts, specifically Acts 2, where we encounter the remarkable account of the Day of Pentecost. On that momentous day, as the disciples were gathered in Jerusalem, something extraordinary occurred. "When the day of Pentecost arrived, they were all together in one place. And suddenly there came from heaven a sound like a mighty rushing wind, and it filled the entire house where they were sitting. And divided tongues as of fire appeared to them and rested on each one of them. And they were all filled with the Holy Spirit and began to speak in other tongues as the Spirit gave them utterance" This event serves as a foundational example of speaking in tongues, highlighting its supernatural nature and its connection to the outpouring of the Holy Spirit. It's a vivid demonstration of God's presence and power, echoing the promise made by Jesus in Mark 16:17: "And these signs will accompany those who believe: in my name, they will cast out demons; they will speak in new tongues."

But our journey doesn't stop there. We also explore the teachings of the Apostle Paul in 1 Corinthians 12-14, where he provides valuable insights into the purpose and practice of speaking in tongues within the context of the Church. Paul speaks of tongues as a spiritual gift that edifies the individual believer and can serve as a means of communication between the believer and God. He encourages the responsible exercise of this gift for the edification of the Church, emphasizing love as the guiding principle in its use.

As we delve into these passages and others, we'll gain a comprehensive understanding of the scriptural basis for speaking in tongues. These biblical references serve as signposts on our journey, helping us navigate the waters of this unique spiritual gift. They provide a solid foundation upon which we can build our understanding of speaking in tongues and its role in the Spirit-filled life, guiding us towards a deeper appreciation of this powerful and mysterious gift.

Our biblical exploration continues with 1 Corinthians 14, where the Apostle Paul further elucidates the purpose and orderliness of speaking in tongues in the context of the Church. He emphasizes the importance of intelligible speech, saying, "For if I pray in a tongue, my spirit prays but my mind is unfruitful. What am I to do? I will pray with my spirit, but I will pray with my mind also; I will sing praise with my spirit, but I will sing with my mind also" (1 Corinthians 14:14-15). Paul's guidance underscores the dual nature of this gift—an intimate communication with God and a means of edifying the body of believers.

Additionally, Mark 16:17-18 reminds us of Jesus' promise that speaking in new tongues would be one of the signs accompanying believers. This promise echoes the supernatural dimension of speaking in tongues, reinforcing its authenticity as a spiritual gift bestowed by the Holy Spirit.

Through these biblical references, we gain a holistic understanding of speaking in tongues—a gift that bridges the human and divine realms, facilitating a unique form of communication between believers and their Creator. As we navigate the pages ahead, we'll explore the multifaceted dimensions of this gift, unraveling its mysteries, and appreciating its role in the Spirit-filled life. It is a journey of discovery that invites us to embrace the fullness of this spiritual gift and its profound connection to our faith journey.

═══════

Discovering the Gift of Tongues: Jeremiah's Journey to Deeper Faith

Meet Jeremiah, a thoughtful man in his late 40s, known for his dedication to his family, his community, and his faith. Raised in a traditional church, Jeremiah had always approached his beliefs with reverence but kept his spiritual experiences within safe boundaries. Yet, he sometimes felt that his prayers lacked depth, like there was something just out of reach, an aspect of faith that remained unexplored. The idea of speaking in tongues seemed distant to him—something he saw in the Bible but considered mysterious and maybe even impractical. But recently, he felt a stirring in his heart, a sense that God was calling him to go deeper, to step beyond the comfort zone he'd created in his spiritual life.

One Sunday, Jeremiah attended a small group Bible study focused on the book of Acts. As they reached the passage on Pentecost in Acts 2, he felt an undeniable pull as they read about the disciples being filled with the Holy Spirit and speaking in tongues. The room seemed to grow still as he imagined himself there among the disciples, feeling the rushing wind and hearing the words flowing from the Spirit. A thought came to him: Could this be what I've been missing? Could this kind of communion with God truly be accessible to me?

A few weeks later, Jeremiah found himself in his study, grappling with his longing for a deeper spiritual connection. He remembered the promises of Jesus in Mark 16:17 and the encouragement of Paul in 1 Corinthians 14. For the first time, he felt ready to ask God for this gift. Alone in his room, he prayed quietly, "Lord, if this gift is truly from You, if speaking in tongues can bring me closer to You, I'm open to receiving it."

In that moment, Jeremiah felt a warmth fill the room, a presence so real that tears filled his eyes. He spoke quietly at first, then words he didn't understand began to flow from him, gentle but powerful. He felt as though he had tapped into a wellspring of love and grace beyond anything he had known. It was a moment of surrender and peace, an experience he could barely describe. It was as if his spirit was speaking directly to God without the limitations of language.

From that day, Jeremiah's prayer life changed dramatically. His time with God felt richer, more intimate. His family and friends noticed a new confidence in him, a quiet joy that seemed to color everything he did. He found strength to face challenges with a peace he hadn't known before, knowing he could turn to this deep, Spirit-filled connection whenever he needed it.

Jeremiah's experience with the gift of tongues taught him that this biblical practice wasn't just for distant times or extraordinary people—it was a gift available to every believer willing to seek it. His journey reflects the value of stepping into the unknown and trusting God to deepen our faith in ways beyond understanding. For Jeremiah and countless others, speaking in tongues became not just a spiritual tool but a bridge to a richer, more authentic relationship with God, one that continues to shape him every day.

———————

The Purpose and Benefits of Speaking in Tongues

In this chapter, we embark on a quest to uncover the profound purposes and abundant benefits of speaking in tongues—a gift often shrouded in mystery but overflowing with spiritual richness. To truly grasp the significance of this gift, we must journey both within ourselves and within the context of the Church, exploring its personal and corporate dimensions.

First and foremost, speaking in tongues fosters a deeper and more intimate relationship with God. It's a unique form of communication between the believer and their Creator, a direct line of spiritual dialogue. The Apostle Paul, in his letter to the Corinthians, explains that when we speak in tongues, "we speak mysteries in the Spirit" (1 Corinthians 14:2). These mysteries are like hidden treasures, allowing us to communicate with God on a profound level that transcends the limitations of our human understanding. It's as if we are engaging in a heavenly conversation, drawing closer to the heart of God.

Moreover, speaking in tongues is a powerful tool for personal spiritual growth. Paul continues in 1 Corinthians 14, saying that when we pray in tongues, our spirits are engaged, even though our minds may not fully comprehend. This spiritual exercise strengthens our inner being, building us up in faith and empowering us to walk in the Spirit. It's like a spiritual workout that keeps our faith muscles strong and vibrant.

But speaking in tongues is not just about personal enrichment; it also plays a vital role in the corporate life of the Church. In the book of Acts, we see the disciples speaking in tongues on the Day of Pentecost, and the result is astonishing: people from various nations hear them in their own languages, and many come to faith (Acts 2:4-11). This illustrates one of the corporate benefits of speaking in tongues—the ability to transcend language barriers and reach hearts with the gospel message.

Additionally, speaking in tongues is a powerful form of worship. When we worship in tongues, we engage in pure, unfiltered adoration of God, as described in 1 Corinthians 14:15: "I will sing praise with my spirit." It's a form of worship that goes beyond the confines of language, allowing our spirits to soar in the presence of the Almighty.

Furthermore, speaking in tongues is a potent weapon in spiritual warfare. In Ephesians 6:18, Paul encourages believers to "pray at all times in the Spirit," highlighting the role of tongues in our spiritual battles. It's a way of aligning ourselves with the Holy Spirit's guidance and power, allowing us to stand firm against the schemes of the enemy.

As we journey through this exploration of the purposes and benefits of speaking in tongues, we'll uncover a treasure trove of spiritual riches—a gift that deepens our relationship with God, fosters our personal growth, enriches our worship, and equips us for spiritual warfare. It's a gift that continues to have a profound impact on the lives of believers and the edification of the Church, showcasing the enduring power and relevance of the Holy Spirit's work in our lives today.

Furthermore, speaking in tongues serves as a powerful channel for intercessory prayer. Romans 8:26 reminds us that "the Spirit helps us in our weakness. For we do not know what to pray for as we ought, but the Spirit himself intercedes for us with groanings too deep for words." Speaking in tongues, as a manifestation of the Spirit's presence, allows us to partner with the Holy Spirit in our prayers. When words fail us, the Spirit intercedes on our behalf, bringing our deepest needs and desires before the throne of grace.

In the corporate life of the Church, the gift of speaking in tongues takes on an even greater significance. Paul emphasizes the importance of orderly worship in 1 Corinthians 14:26-33, highlighting the need for interpretation when tongues are spoken in a public gathering. When exercised in this manner, tongues can contribute to the edification of the entire congregation. It can serve as a sign to unbelievers, as seen in 1 Corinthians 14:22, where Paul states that "tongues are a sign not for believers but for unbelievers." This sign can pique the curiosity of those who are seeking spiritual truth and lead them to a deeper encounter with God.

Speaking in tongues also fosters unity within the Church, as it transcends language and cultural barriers. The diversity of tongues within the body of believers is a reflection of God's inclusive love for all nations and peoples, as we see in

Revelation 7:9-10, where a multitude from every nation, tribe, and language worships before the throne.

In times of corporate worship and prayer, the presence of tongues can create an atmosphere of spiritual sensitivity, allowing the Holy Spirit to move freely among the congregation. This can lead to moments of prophetic revelation, words of knowledge, and the manifestation of other spiritual gifts that edify and encourage the Church.

As we delve deeper into the multifaceted purposes and benefits of speaking in tongues, we discover that this gift is not confined to a single role but encompasses a rich tapestry of functions. It deepens our connection with God, fosters personal growth, enriches our worship, equips us for spiritual warfare, and enhances the corporate life of the Church. It is a gift that continues to demonstrate its enduring power and relevance in the Spirit-filled life, inviting us to embrace its full potential for the glory of God and the edification of His people.

―――――――

Joy's Journey to Deeper
Faith and Boldness

Meet Joy, a passionate believer in her late 30s with an energetic spirit and an unwavering dedication to her church and family. Though deeply committed to her faith, she often found herself feeling spiritually stagnant, yearning for a deeper connection with God but uncertain how to reach it. Despite years of faithful service and personal devotion, she carried a quiet ache for something more—a longing for a more intimate, transformative relationship with God.

One Sunday, during a sermon on spiritual gifts, Joy listened intently as her pastor spoke about speaking in tongues as a personal and communal gift of the Holy Spirit. It was a concept Joy had often heard about but felt hesitant to explore. However, as she sat in her pew, she felt a gentle nudge, almost like an invitation. Her heart raced with both excitement and apprehension. Could this be the key to deepening her faith?

That night, Joy sat alone in her living room, replaying the pastor's words in her mind. She took a deep breath and prayed, "Lord, if this gift is truly from You, if it will bring me closer to You and empower me to serve, I want to receive it." She closed her eyes and began to pray quietly, inviting the Holy Spirit to fill her. Gradually, she felt a warmth settle in her heart, and unfamiliar words began to flow, softly at first, but with increasing clarity. Joy realized she was speaking in tongues. It was a deeply personal moment; unlike any prayer she had known before—a direct connection with God that transcended words.

In the weeks that followed, Joy noticed a transformation in her life. Her times of prayer felt richer, more profound. Speaking in tongues had become a private language of intimacy between her and God, a way of praying when words seemed insufficient. She found herself uplifted and energized; her faith strengthened. There were moments when she felt a surge of courage, allowing her to step out in boldness to share her faith, something she had always hesitated to do.

One day during a church service, Joy felt led to pray in tongues quietly during worship. She felt a sense of unity with her fellow believers, a spiritual connection that went beyond spoken words. After the service, a new attendee approached her, sharing how he had been deeply moved by the worship and sensed something powerful in the atmosphere. Joy realized that speaking in tongues had not only deepened her connection with God but was now impacting others, creating an environment where the Holy Spirit could touch lives.

As Joy continued to grow in her faith, she discovered other benefits of this gift. During a difficult season when a friend faced illness, Joy found solace in praying in tongues, knowing that even when she couldn't find the right words, the Holy Spirit was interceding on her behalf. Her prayer life became more vibrant and effective, filled with peace even in challenging times.

Joy's journey with speaking in tongues became a testimony of God's power working in her life, enriching her faith, strengthening her spirit, and connecting her with others in a profound way. Her story reminds us that the Holy Spirit's gifts are available to all who seek them, not only for personal growth but for the edification of the Church and as a channel of God's love to those around us. Joy's experience has left her heart full and her faith unshaken, a reminder that God's gifts carry real, life-changing power for all who are willing to receive.

———

Contemporary Perspectives and Experiences

In this chapter, we take a step closer to understanding the rich tapestry of speaking in tongues by exploring contemporary perspectives and real-life experiences of individuals who have encountered this extraordinary gift. Their stories provide a glimpse into the diverse ways in which speaking in tongues continues to shape modern Christian life, emphasizing its relevance and profound impact in today's spiritual landscape.

Meet Harlow, a young woman whose journey of faith led her to a Pentecostal church where speaking in tongues was a common practice. At first, she was apprehensive, not fully comprehending the gift. However, one Sunday during worship, something remarkable happened. As she surrendered herself to God's presence, a rush of unfamiliar words flowed from her lips. It was as if a heavenly language had been unlocked within her, a language she couldn't understand with her mind but felt deeply in her spirit. Harlow's experience aligns with the Apostle Paul's words in 1 Corinthians 14:2: "For one who speaks in a tongue speaks not to men but to God; for no one understands him, but he utters mysteries in the Spirit." Through speaking in tongues, Harlow found a way to communicate with God on a profound level that transcended human limitations.

Jude's story takes us into the realm of personal empowerment and spiritual growth. As a young believer, he had often struggled with doubt and uncertainty about his faith. Seeking a deeper connection with God, he attended a charismatic conference where the practice of speaking in tongues was emphasized. During a powerful moment of prayer, he felt an overwhelming surge of God's presence, and words in a new language began to flow from his heart. It was as if a floodgate of faith had opened within him, strengthening his relationship with God and igniting a passion for Scripture and prayer. Jude's experience echoes the Apostle Paul's words in Jude 1:20: "But you, beloved, building yourselves up in your most holy faith and praying in the Holy Spirit."

Jada's testimony illustrates the communal aspect of speaking in tongues within the Church. As a member of a charismatic congregation, she witnessed how the practice of speaking in tongues contributed to the unity and spiritual vitality of the community. During times of corporate worship and prayer, the congregation would often engage in spontaneous prayer in tongues, creating an atmosphere of spiritual sensitivity and intimacy. This practice enhanced their collective experience of God's presence and led to moments of prophetic revelation and encouragement, as seen in 1 Corinthians 14:26: "What then, brothers? When you come together, each one has a hymn, a lesson, a revelation, a tongue,

or an interpretation. Let all things be done for building up."
Jada's story demonstrates how speaking in tongues can foster
a sense of spiritual unity and deeper connection within the
Church.

These contemporary testimonies serve as living evidence
of the enduring relevance and transformative power of
speaking in tongues in today's spiritual landscape. They remind
us that this gift is not a relic of the past but a vibrant reality,
offering believers a unique channel of communication with
God, personal empowerment, spiritual growth, and unity
within the body of Christ. As we journey forward, let these
stories inspire us to embrace the fullness of the Spirit-filled life,
recognizing that the gift of speaking in tongues continues to
play a vital role in the modern Christian experience.

In the tapestry of contemporary Christian life, the diverse
testimonies we've encountered serve as vibrant threads,
weaving together a mosaic of experiences and insights into the
gift of speaking in tongues. These stories are not isolated
incidents but are part of a broader narrative—a narrative of
believers who have encountered the living God through this
extraordinary gift.

Harlow's experience reflects the intimate communion that
speaking in tongues can bring—an intimate, mysterious
dialogue between the believer and their Creator. It mirrors the
Apostle Paul's assertion that when we speak in tongues, we
speak mysteries in the Spirit. It's a language of the heart, a

language that transcends human understanding, enabling us to connect with God on a profound level.

Jude's journey showcases the personal empowerment and spiritual growth that speaking in tongues can catalyze. His story resonates with those moments when doubt gives way to faith, uncertainty yields to assurance, and the Word of God comes alive in our hearts. It embodies the Apostle Jude's exhortation to build ourselves up in our most holy faith, praying in the Holy Spirit.

Jada's testimony highlights the communal dimension of speaking in tongues—a gift that enhances the unity and spiritual vibrancy of the Church. It echoes the Apostle Paul's teaching that when believers gather, each one has something to contribute for the building up of the body of Christ. In the midst of corporate worship and prayer, speaking in tongues creates an atmosphere where the Holy Spirit can move freely, leading to moments of prophetic revelation and edification.

As we reflect on these contemporary perspectives and experiences, we are reminded that speaking in tongues is not a relic of a bygone era but a living reality—an invitation to encounter the living God, to experience personal transformation, and to contribute to the unity and vitality of the Church.

These testimonies encourage us to approach the gift of speaking in tongues with an open heart and a receptive spirit, recognizing its multifaceted roles in our faith journey. They beckon us to explore the depths of the Spirit-filled life, where the supernatural and the ordinary converge, where mysteries are unveiled, and where God's presence is tangibly felt. In the chapters ahead, we will continue to unravel the intricate threads of this gift, discovering its manifold dimensions and uncovering its potential for our personal spiritual growth and the flourishing of the Church.

Jesse's Journey of Faith and Transformation Through Speaking in Tongues

Jesse, a thoughtful and reserved man in his late 40s, had always been a steady churchgoer. He loved God, yet often felt something was missing in his spiritual journey. He longed for a deeper connection, one that would feel tangible and personal. Over the years, he'd heard about speaking in tongues but was unsure about it. He saw it as something mystical, something other people experienced—until an encounter changed his life.

One Saturday evening, Jesse attended a worship service at a friend's charismatic church. During a moment of quiet prayer, he felt an intense warmth flood over him, as if he was wrapped in a divine embrace. In that moment, words began to rise up within him—words he didn't understand but felt powerfully in his heart. Hesitantly, he let them flow. It felt strange, yet freeing, like an expression of his spirit reaching beyond the limitations of language.

This experience became a turning point. Jesse found himself transformed, not just in that moment, but in his daily walk with God. When he prayed in tongues, he felt a closeness to God that he'd never experienced before. It was as if he had discovered a new way to commune with his Creator. Jesse's faith grew deeper, rooted in a tangible sense of God's presence. His experience resonates with the Apostle Paul's teaching in 1 Corinthians 14:2: "For anyone who speaks in a tongue does not speak to people but to God. Indeed, no one understands them; they utter mysteries by the Spirit."

What surprised Jesse most was the way this newfound intimacy with God impacted other areas of his life. His prayers took on new meaning, his personal devotions became richer, and he discovered a confidence to share his faith with others. The gift he'd received strengthened his spirit in a way that felt like a personal conversation with God, refreshing him like streams of living water.

One Sunday morning, Jesse was asked to join a prayer group at church. As they prayed together, he felt moved to quietly pray in tongues. The presence of God seemed to fill the room, creating a powerful sense of unity and reverence among the group. Fellow members later shared that they'd experienced God's peace and clarity in their prayers that morning, feeling strengthened by a sense of His nearness.

Jesse's story is a testament to the transformative power of speaking in tongues, not only as a deeply personal communion with God but as a way to strengthen faith, inspire confidence, and foster unity in the Church. His experience reminds us that the Holy Spirit's gifts are not relics of the past but are alive and active in the lives of believers today, empowering us to live a Spirit-filled life of purpose and connection.

Conclusion

As we bring Chapter 4 to a close, we find ourselves on the brink of a profound revelation—a revelation that has taken us deep into the heart of speaking in tongues, a gift that has fascinated and captivated believers for generations. Throughout this chapter, we've explored the intricate tapestry of this phenomenon, unveiling its biblical roots, understanding its diverse purposes, and hearing the voices of those who have encountered its transformative power in the here and now.

Speaking in tongues, often described as the "language of heaven," has emerged as a vibrant, living aspect of the Spirit-filled life. It's a gift that transcends the ordinary, inviting us to explore a richer, more vibrant experience of faith—a journey where words may fail, but the Spirit's presence abounds. It's a language that allows us to converse with the divine, to deepen our connection with God, and to become vessels of His power.

As we've delved deeper into this gift, we've not only uncovered its mysteries but also discovered its profound relevance in the modern Christian experience. We've learned that speaking in tongues fosters intimacy with God, fuels personal growth, enriches our worship, and equips us for spiritual warfare. It's a gift that has the power to unite the body of believers, to transcend language barriers, and to create an atmosphere where the Holy Spirit moves freely.

But our journey is far from over. In the chapters ahead, we will continue to unravel the intricate threads of the Spirit-filled life, exploring its manifold dimensions, and uncovering its potential for personal spiritual growth and the flourishing of the Church. So, as we conclude this chapter, let the echoes of these diverse voices from eternity resonate in your heart, for they remind us that the gift of speaking in tongues is not a relic of the past but a vibrant, living reality—an invitation to encounter the living God, to experience personal transformation, and to contribute to the unity and vitality of the Church. The journey continues, and the mysteries of the Spirit-filled life await our exploration.

CHAPTER FIVE

Public vs. Private Utterances: Navigating the Different Expressions of Tongues

"But in the church I would rather speak five intelligible words to instruct others than ten thousand words in a tongue."
— 1 CORINTHIANS 14:19 NIV

As we step into this chapter, we are invited to explore one of the most profound and enigmatic gifts given by the Holy Spirit: the gift of speaking in tongues. This spiritual gift, often mysterious and misunderstood, is deeply embedded in the life of the Spirit-filled believer, offering layers of purpose and meaning that extend from private moments of prayer to the shared experiences of worship within the community of faith. In exploring this sacred gift, we uncover a language that transcends the limits of human speech and expresses the depths of our hearts in ways that only God can truly understand. It is here, in the delicate balance between private and public expressions, that we find the dual dimensions of speaking in tongues—a personal language of intimacy and a public display of unity that speaks to the diversity and beauty of the body of Christ.

The private utterance of tongues, or the personal prayer language, is an invitation to enter a uniquely intimate space with God. In this sacred communion, the believer is empowered to speak beyond their understanding, expressing the inexpressible, and reaching into the very heart of God. When we turn to Scripture, we see that this gift is not merely a phenomenon of the past but a present reality that offers us direct access to the mind of the Spirit. The Apostle Paul, in Romans 8:26, describes this experience with profound insight: "Likewise, the Spirit helps us in our weakness. For we do not know what to pray for as we ought, but the Spirit himself intercedes for us with groanings too deep for words." In this private language of prayer, the Holy Spirit becomes our intercessor, taking the simple and often incomplete prayers of our hearts and translating them into a heavenly language that aligns perfectly with God's will. This personal expression of tongues allows us to surrender our deepest needs, desires, and praises into the hands of the Holy Spirit, who, in turn, brings them before the throne of grace.

But this gift is not only for the private realm; it also has a powerful role within the public life of the Church. In the community of believers, speaking in tongues takes on a different dimension, becoming a testimony to the unity and diversity of the body of Christ. The Apostle Paul's teachings in 1 Corinthians 14 illuminate the purpose of this gift in public worship, reminding us that speaking in tongues, when accompanied by interpretation, is meant to build up the Church. Paul writes, "What then, brothers? When you come together, each one has a hymn, a lesson, a revelation, a tongue, or an interpretation. Let all things be done for building up" (1 Corinthians 14:26). This verse reveals the heart of public worship: a setting where each spiritual gift contributes to the encouragement, strengthening, and edification of the body as a whole.

In public worship, speaking in tongues is more than a personal experience—it is a corporate act that requires sensitivity, order, and reverence. It is an expression that can bridge linguistic and cultural divides, reflecting the unity of the body of Christ even amidst our diversity. However, the Apostle Paul also offers caution and guidelines, emphasizing that God is not a God of confusion but of peace (1 Corinthians 14:33). For this reason, when tongues are spoken in a corporate setting, they are to be followed by interpretation. This essential practice allows the congregation to understand and receive the message conveyed, ensuring that the gift is used in a way that benefits all present. Through the interpretation, the Spirit's message is brought from the spiritual realm into the understanding of the natural, allowing believers to be encouraged and strengthened in their faith. Paul further affirms this principle by saying, "Now I want you all to speak in tongues, but even more to prophesy. The one who prophesies is greater than the one who speaks in tongues unless someone interprets, so that the church may be built up" (1 Corinthians 14:5). This underscores that, while speaking in tongues is a beautiful and powerful gift, it must be balanced with the needs of the congregation for edification and understanding.

To deepen our understanding of speaking in tongues, we must also look at the role of the gift of interpretation. The interpretation of tongues serves as a bridge, translating the message from the spiritual language of tongues into the natural language of the congregation. This gift allows the Church to benefit from the message that the Holy Spirit conveys through tongues, transforming it from a private expression to a corporate experience. When tongues and interpretation operate together in a congregational setting, they create a dynamic interplay that reveals the heart and mind of God in real-time, bringing clarity and insight to the Church. In 1 Corinthians 12:10, Paul mentions this gift as one of the many spiritual gifts given for the common good, stating, "To another the working of miracles, to another prophecy, to another the ability to distinguish between spirits, to another various kinds of tongues, to another the interpretation of tongues." This passage highlights that interpretation is not an afterthought but a critical gift that ensures the message of tongues is understood and received by all.

The gift of interpretation also holds significance in private expressions of speaking in tongues. When we pray in tongues during personal devotion, there may be times when the Holy Spirit reveals insights, direction, or encouragement that can only be fully grasped through interpretation. In these moments, the interpretation of tongues serves to bring understanding and clarity to the Spirit's message, allowing the believer to apply it more effectively in their life. As Paul encourages in 1 Corinthians 14:13, "Therefore, one who speaks in a tongue should pray that he may interpret." By seeking the gift of interpretation, we acknowledge that the Holy Spirit's messages are too precious to remain hidden; they are meant to be understood, cherished, and applied.

As we navigate the expressions of speaking in tongues, both in private prayer and public worship, we see that this gift is a profound demonstration of God's desire to communicate with His people. Whether used in the quiet solitude of personal devotion or the vibrant tapestry of corporate worship, the gift of tongues is an invitation to enter deeper into the mysteries of God. It reminds us that we are connected to a supernatural reality that goes beyond what we can see or understand with our natural minds. In private, it is a language of intimacy, drawing us closer to God and allowing the Holy Spirit to intercede for us in ways beyond our comprehension. In public, it is a testament to the unity and diversity of the body of Christ, a visible and audible reminder that we are part of a global family, united by the same Spirit.

In this chapter, we will explore these expressions of tongues in greater depth, examining the biblical foundations, the purpose, and the principles that guide their use. We will discuss how to navigate the private and public dimensions of this gift responsibly, understanding that both are essential to a Spirit-filled life. May this journey open your heart to the richness of speaking in tongues, whether in the quiet moments of prayer or in the shared experience of worship. As we engage with this gift, let us be open to the ways the Holy Spirit may speak to us, guide us, and draw us ever closer to the heart of God. In both the seen and unseen expressions, may we find ourselves immersed in the Spirit's love, wisdom, and power, living out a faith that speaks the language of heaven.

The Private Language of Prayer

In the quiet moments of our faith journey, there exists a profound and intimate language—a language that transcends our earthly limitations and pierces the heavens. It's the language of speaking in tongues as a personal prayer language, a gift bestowed by the Holy Spirit for our deepest communion with God.

In Romans 8:26, we find a powerful affirmation of this unique form of prayer: "Likewise, the Spirit helps us in our weakness. For we do not know what to pray for as we ought, but the Spirit himself intercedes for us with groanings too deep for words." These groanings too deep for words, these utterances that flow from our spirits when we speak in tongues, become a channel through which the Holy Spirit intercedes on our behalf. It's as if the Spirit takes our feeble, imperfect prayers and transforms them into something profound, something that resonates with the very heart of God.

When we speak in tongues privately, we enter into a sacred space of connection with the divine. It's a form of prayer where words, shaped by our limited human understanding, yield to the Spirit's perfect intercession. It's a language of the heart, a language of surrender, a language that says, "Lord, I trust You to communicate my deepest needs, desires, and praises to You." It's a language of faith, acknowledging that our Heavenly Father comprehends even our unspoken longings.

In these private moments of communion, speaking in tongues becomes a transformative force. It deepens our prayer life, drawing us into a deeper relationship with God. It's as if we're peering into the depths of His love, experiencing a level of intimacy that transcends mere words. The Apostle Paul, in 1 Corinthians 14:2, captures the essence of this experience: "For one who speaks in a tongue speaks not to men but to God; for no one understands him, but he utters mysteries in the Spirit." It's a journey into the realm of divine mysteries—a realm where we're held in the embrace of our Heavenly Father, where we're known and loved in our most vulnerable moments.

As we navigate the landscape of this personal prayer language, we discover that speaking in tongues isn't just a gift; it's a profound expression of trust and surrender. It's an invitation to draw near to God in the quiet recesses of our hearts, to entrust our deepest concerns to the Spirit's intercession, and to experience the transformative power of communion with the divine. It's a sacred language, a bridge between the earthly and the heavenly, an unseen force that draws us closer to the One who hears even our unspoken words.

In the tapestry of our faith, this private language of prayer serves as a direct line of communication with the divine—a line unburdened by the limitations of our human vocabulary. It's in these moments of speaking in tongues that we express our trust in the Holy Spirit's guidance, allowing Him to carry the weight of our petitions, our thanksgiving, and our deepest groanings.

Consider the words of the Apostle Paul in 1 Corinthians 14:15: "What am I to do? I will pray with my spirit, but I will pray with my mind also; I will sing praise with my spirit, but I will sing with my mind also." Here, we see the harmony between the language of the spirit and the language of the mind. Speaking in tongues becomes a unique dimension of our prayer life, coexisting alongside our cognitive prayers. It enriches our worship experience, allowing us to express our adoration, gratitude, and surrender in a way that transcends the boundaries of human language.

As we engage in this private language of prayer, we are drawn into a sacred rhythm—a rhythm where our hearts beat in harmony with the heartbeat of our Heavenly Father. It's a rhythm of surrender and trust, of listening and responding, of drawing near and receiving divine revelation. It's in this intimate space that we find solace, renewal, and a profound sense of connection with the divine.

The private language of speaking in tongues, as a personal prayer language, beckons us to embrace the fullness of our spiritual journey —a journey where words may falter, but the Spirit speaks fluently. It's an invitation to deepen our communion with God, to surrender our deepest concerns into His capable hands, and to experience the transformative power of intimacy with the One who knows us intimately. As we continue our exploration of speaking in tongues, let us cherish the sacred moments of this personal prayer language, for within them, we encounter the unseen force of divine power that draws us ever closer to the heart of our Creator.

———————

Ingrid's Quiet Journey with the Private Language of Prayer

Ingrid, a dedicated teacher in her early thirties, had a deep love for her students and her work, yet often felt emotionally and spiritually drained. Life was busy, full of obligations and concerns she brought to God in prayer every day, yet something felt missing—a way to reach beyond her worries, to truly connect with Him. She longed for more depth, for a more intimate way to express her deepest needs, but felt words alone were insufficient.

One evening after a particularly trying day, she sat alone in her living room, searching for peace. With a heart weary of words, she simply began to pray. Then, unexpectedly, she felt a gentle prompting in her spirit—a nudge to let go and allow the Holy Spirit to intercede for her. Softly, sounds she didn't understand began to form on her lips. At first, it felt unusual, even awkward, but soon, a comforting calm washed over her, and she realized she was speaking to God in a new way, bypassing her own thoughts and limitations.

In that quiet moment, she was reminded of Romans 8:26: "The Spirit himself intercedes for us with groanings too deep for words." Ingrid's private prayer language became her haven of surrender, her way of saying, "Lord, you know my heart better than I do. Take my burdens and let Your Spirit speak for me."

This new, private way of praying in tongues transformed Ingrid's daily life. As she let herself speak to God through this unique language, she found solace that reached beyond her usual prayers. It was like lifting the weight off her own shoulders, letting the Holy Spirit communicate her deepest concerns. And gradually, her personal prayer language became her sanctuary, where she found rest and renewal.

Ingrid's experience is a powerful reminder of the intimacy available in a private prayer language. It serves as an invitation to any believer searching for a deeper connection with God— a way to engage with the Holy Spirit that reaches beyond words, into the mystery of God's heart.

Public Expression in Corporate Worship

As we gather in the sanctuary, amidst the harmonious blend of voices and the stirring melodies of worship, there exists a unique expression—an expression that has the power to elevate our collective experience of God's presence. It is the expression of speaking in tongues within the context of public worship, a gift bestowed by the Holy Spirit for the edification of the Church.

In 1 Corinthians 14:26, the Apostle Paul offers insight into the purpose of this gift in congregational settings: "What then, brothers? When you come together, each one has a hymn, a lesson, a revelation, a tongue, or an interpretation. Let all things be done for building up." Here, Paul emphasizes the importance of orderly worship, where the diverse spiritual gifts, including speaking in tongues and interpretation, work together for the building up of the Church.

In these public expressions of speaking in tongues, there is an opportunity for believers to engage in corporate worship that transcends linguistic and cultural boundaries. It becomes a reflection of the unity within the body of Christ, where the Spirit's presence moves freely, bringing forth spiritual gifts for the common good. However, it is essential that guidelines and biblical principles be observed to ensure responsible exercise of this gift.

One key principle to bear in mind is found in 1 Corinthians 14:33: "For God is not a God of confusion but of peace." Therefore, when speaking in tongues is practiced in public worship, it should be done in an orderly manner, with the understanding that an interpretation should follow. The gift of interpretation of tongues is essential to ensure that the congregation can benefit from the message conveyed through tongues.

This practice aligns with Paul's exhortation in 1 Corinthians 14:5: "Now I want you all to speak in tongues, but even more to prophesy. The one who prophesies is greater than the one who speaks in tongues unless someone interprets so that the church may be built up."

While the public expression of speaking in tongues can enhance our corporate worship experience, it can also pose challenges and misconceptions. It is essential to address these concerns sensitively and biblically. Some may be unfamiliar with this gift, and clear explanations can help demystify its purpose and role within the Church. Additionally, fostering an atmosphere of reverence and understanding in congregational settings is vital to ensure that all members can participate in worship with a sense of unity and edification.

In the realm of public worship, the expression of speaking in tongues invites us to embrace the diversity of spiritual gifts within the body of Christ. It reminds us of the unity we share in our faith, transcending language barriers and cultural differences. When practiced in accordance with biblical principles, it contributes to the edification of the Church, allowing the Spirit's presence to move mightily in our midst. So, let us approach the public expression of speaking in tongues with reverence, understanding, and a commitment to building up the body of Christ.

In the vibrant tapestry of congregational worship, the expression of speaking in tongues stands as a testament to the diversity of spiritual gifts and the unity of the body of Christ. It is a reflection of the Apostle Paul's vision in 1 Corinthians 12:4-7: "Now there are varieties of gifts, but the same Spirit; and there are varieties of service, but the same Lord; and there are varieties of activities, but it is the same God who empowers them all in everyone. To each is given the manifestation of the Spirit for the common good."

When practiced responsibly, speaking in tongues in public worship serves as a beautiful expression of the Holy Spirit's presence, enriching our corporate experience with the divine. It reminds us that we are part of a global family of believers, transcending linguistic and cultural boundaries, united by our faith in Christ. It fosters an atmosphere of expectancy, where the supernatural meets the ordinary, and where the Spirit's guidance is sought and cherished.

However, it's important to address potential challenges and misconceptions that may arise in these contexts. Some may question the purpose of speaking in tongues or be unfamiliar with its biblical foundation. It's our responsibility to provide clear explanations and scriptural support for this gift. Moreover, we must emphasize the need for orderly worship, ensuring that interpretations follow instances of speaking in tongues so that the entire congregation may benefit.

As we navigate the delicate balance of public expression, let us do so with an understanding heart and a commitment to edification. Let us foster an atmosphere where the diversity of spiritual gifts can flourish, where the unity of the body of Christ is celebrated, and where the Spirit's presence is evident. In the realm of public worship, speaking in tongues becomes a powerful means through which we draw near to God as a community, collectively edifying one another and offering our praises to the King of kings. It is a sacred expression, a testament to our faith, and a reminder that the Spirit-filled life is a life lived in unity, diversity, and reverence for the God who speaks in many tongues.

———

A Church Service Transformed

At First Assembly Church, Sunday worship had always been a time of song, prayer, and preaching. But one morning, as the congregation gathered in the sanctuary, there was a new and reverent expectation in the air. Daphne, a longtime member and known for her heart of service, was praying quietly, waiting on God. She had recently learned about the gift of speaking in tongues in a small group study and was curious but cautious, unsure how this gift fit into her own life and the broader church setting. She had prayed for clarity and a sign of how God might use her in this way.

That morning, as worship concluded, Daphne felt a strong nudge to speak in tongues. She wrestled internally, hesitant about how it would be received, but as the sense grew stronger, she yielded to it, letting words flow from her spirit. The language was unfamiliar, but her heart was aligned with a clear reverence and purpose. As she spoke, the congregation listened quietly, many sensing something powerful was unfolding. Immediately after, a church elder stood up, feeling led to interpret. His words, translated from Daphne's utterance, spoke of God's love for the congregation and a call for each person to draw nearer to Him in trust and unity.

The effect was profound. Many congregants later shared how they felt seen and loved by God in a deeply personal way through this message. Some, experiencing corporate speaking in tongues for the first time, expressed that it moved them to a deeper understanding of God's presence and love for each member of the body. Daphne, too, felt transformed—not just by using a gift but by experiencing the Spirit's unity and purpose for His Church.

This moment of public tongues and interpretation brought a new sense of community, unity, and reverence. It showed the congregation the richness of diversity in spiritual gifts, echoing Paul's words in 1 Corinthians 12: "To each is given the manifestation of the Spirit for the common good." Through this experience, First Assembly saw firsthand the importance of speaking in tongues in corporate worship and the impact it can have when used with respect, love, and orderly practice. The atmosphere of the church shifted, becoming one of openness to the Spirit's movement and an enhanced commitment to unity and encouragement.

Daphne's story reflects the beauty and purpose of public expression in corporate worship, reminding us of the Holy Spirit's desire to build up the Church, foster unity, and lead every believer into a deeper relationship with God.

=====

Interpreting Tongues: The Role of the Gift of interpretation

Within the tapestry of spiritual gifts, one stands as a companion to the gift of speaking in tongues—the gift of interpretation of tongues. Like two pieces of a divine puzzle, they fit together, creating a picture of clarity, edification, and unity within the body of Christ.

In 1 Corinthians 12:10, the Apostle Paul introduces us to this complementary gift: "To another the working of miracles, to another prophecy, to another the ability to distinguish between spirits, to another various kinds of tongues, to another the interpretation of tongues." This gift of interpretation is a vital component that brings understanding to the messages conveyed through tongues. It serves as a bridge between the spiritual and the tangible, ensuring that the Church is built up and edified.

Imagine a congregation where the gift of tongues is exercised in a public worship setting, followed by the gift of interpretation. This tandem operation allows the congregation to receive the message conveyed through tongues in a language they understand. It aligns with the Apostle Paul's teaching in 1 Corinthians 14:13: "Therefore, one who speaks in a tongue should pray that he may interpret." This underscores the responsibility of those who speak in tongues to seek the gift of interpretation, recognizing that its purpose is to benefit the entire body.

Moreover, the gift of interpretation plays a significant role in private expressions of speaking in tongues. When individuals pray in tongues during their personal devotions, they often receive insights and messages from the Holy Spirit. These personal messages can be a source of encouragement, direction, or revelation. However, to fully grasp the meaning and application of these messages, the gift of interpretation is indispensable.

This harmonious interplay between speaking in tongues and the gift of interpretation deepens our understanding of God's communication with us. Just as we find in 1 Corinthians 14:5, "The one who prophesies is greater than the one who speaks in tongues unless someone interprets, so that the church may be built up." Interpretation ensures that the messages from the Spirit are not hidden or lost in the realm of the supernatural but are made clear and accessible to all.

In the life of the Church, the gift of interpretation brings unity and edification, creating an atmosphere where believers can grow in faith and understanding. When this gift operates effectively, it allows the congregation to receive the wisdom, knowledge, or encouragement that God intends to convey through the messages spoken in tongues.

As we navigate the role of interpretation of tongues, both in private devotion and public worship, let us recognize its significance as a divine catalyst for clarity and edification. It enriches our spiritual experience, allowing us to understand the heart and mind of God, as conveyed through the gift of tongues. It is a gift that fosters unity, deepens faith, and enhances our connection with the divine—the unseen force that speaks through many tongues, all for the glory and edification of His Church.

A Moment of Divine Clarity

At New Hope Community Church, Sunday worship had a different tone that morning. As worship transitioned to prayer, the congregation sensed a heightened anticipation, a readiness for something beyond the usual. Midway through the service, Carlos, a quiet member known for his steadfast faith, began speaking in tongues. The congregation listened intently, many silently praying for insight into what God was communicating.

Adriana, a woman in her fifties who had been part of the church for years, felt a stirring in her heart, a sense that she needed to listen more deeply than ever. She had recently prayed for the gift of interpretation, a gift that fascinated her but which she'd never experienced personally. As Carlos finished, Adriana felt words filling her mind—words she hadn't prepared or planned. With the encouragement of the pastor, she spoke out, interpreting Carlos's message with clarity: "My children, I am with you. I am here to strengthen the weak, to lift the brokenhearted, and to give you courage. Stand firm, for I am your refuge."

A wave of calm and reassurance swept through the congregation. Many, particularly those who had been struggling privately, felt seen and known by God. For Carlos, it was a profound affirmation of his gift. He'd always felt unsure if the gift was helpful to others but now realized its impact, especially when accompanied by interpretation. Adriana was deeply moved, too. She had always wondered if she was hearing God correctly, but this experience showed her that the Spirit's prompting could be trusted.

The congregation later shared that the message spoke to them on multiple levels, uniting them in a shared understanding of God's closeness and compassion. The gift of interpretation, Adriana realized, had brought God's words out of the mystery and into the light, building the faith of everyone present.

The experience taught New Hope Community that the gifts of tongues and interpretation are not isolated abilities but complementary gifts meant to strengthen the body of Christ. For Adriana, Carlos, and the church, it was a clear reminder that God's Spirit is active, drawing His people closer through the gifts He provides. This encounter demonstrated how the gift of interpretation turns mysterious utterances into messages that build up the Church, providing a profound moment of unity, clarity, and divine reassurance.

Conclusion

As we conclude our exploration of public and private expressions of speaking in tongues, we are left with a profound sense of wonder at the Holy Spirit's ability to connect us to God in ways that go beyond human understanding. This spiritual language, whether uttered in the quiet solitude of personal prayer or resounding in the unity of corporate worship, reveals the depths of a divine intimacy designed for each of us. Through the private language of prayer, we access a place of vulnerable surrender, allowing the Holy Spirit to intercede on our behalf with groanings too deep for words. This personal communion with God becomes a sanctuary of strength, comfort, and renewal—a place where our deepest needs are carried to the Father by the Spirit Himself.

In the shared expression of tongues within public worship, we witness a powerful reminder of the unity and diversity within the body of Christ. As Paul outlined, when tongues are accompanied by interpretation, they become a means for building up and encouraging the Church, fostering a corporate atmosphere where each gift plays a part in drawing us closer to God. This public expression is not about individual experience but about collective edification, a celebration of our shared faith and the Spirit's work among us. In this realm, speaking in tongues becomes an anthem of unity, transcending cultural and linguistic divides, inviting us into the heart of a global community.

The gift of interpretation, whether experienced in public or private expressions, serves as a bridge that brings clarity to the mysteries spoken in tongues. It allows us to receive God's wisdom, guidance, and encouragement, transforming what could remain a mystery into a tangible message that we can understand and apply. Together, tongues and interpretation embody the Holy Spirit's desire to reveal God's heart, making the supernatural accessible and meaningful in our everyday lives.

In embracing both the private and public dimensions of speaking in tongues, we are invited to a fuller understanding of the Spirit-filled life. This gift is not merely an expression of ecstatic speech or a distant echo of an ancient tradition; it is a living, dynamic channel through which God continues to move in us and through us. As we practice speaking in tongues, whether in our personal devotion or within the gathering of believers, let us do so with reverence, gratitude, and an openness to the Spirit's guidance.

In a world that often relies on what can be seen and measured, the gift of tongues serves as a reminder of the mysteries of God that invite us to trust, to surrender, and to embrace the unknown. May we move forward with a renewed sense of awe, allowing the Holy Spirit to guide us in both our private communion and our public worship. As we draw near to God in this sacred language, may our hearts be transformed, our faith deepened, and our spirits lifted into the presence of the One who knows us completely and loves us unconditionally.

The Flame Within: Personal Testimonies of the Holy Spirit's Baptism

"But you will receive power when the Holy Spirit comes on you; and you
will be my witnesses in Jerusalem, and in all Judea and Samaria, and to the
ends of the earth." — ACTS 1:8 NIV

Chapter 6, titled "The Flame Within: Personal Testimonies
of the Holy Spirit's Baptism," is an open invitation to
embark on a profoundly inspiring and deeply personal journey
into the heart of the Spirit-filled life. Within these pages lie a
collection of real and heartfelt stories, narratives that bear
witness to the transformative touch of the unseen force of
divine power—the Holy Spirit.

These testimonies are not mere words on pages but living witnesses to the incredible encounters that await those who earnestly seek the presence of the Holy Spirit. In the following chapters, we will walk alongside individuals who have experienced the breathtaking diversity of encounters, profound transformations, and victorious breakthroughs that accompany the Holy Spirit's entrance into their lives.

Each story unfolds as a beacon of hope, a guiding light illuminating the path for those who yearn for a deeper, more intimate connection with the divine. As you turn the pages of this chapter, prepare to be inspired, encouraged, and moved. These testimonies reveal the undeniable reality of the Holy Spirit's baptism and the blazing flame it ignites within the hearts of believers.

The Spirit-filled life is not a distant, elusive concept but a living, breathing reality—one that you, too, can experience. The personal testimonies that follow will serve as companions on your own journey, reminding you that the Holy Spirit is not confined to the pages of Scripture but is a vibrant and active force in the lives of those who open their hearts to His presence. So, let us dive into the tapestry of these testimonies, each thread woven with faith, hope, and the transformative power of the Holy Spirit, as we discover the profound impact of His baptism in the lives of believers.

Diverse Encounters with the Holy Spirit

In the tapestry of faith, each thread tells a unique story—a story of encounters with the Holy Spirit that illuminate the path of believers. As we journey through this chapter, we embark on a voyage of discovery, exploring the diverse encounters people have had with the Holy Spirit. These testimonies are not mere tales but living witnesses to the transformative power of the Holy Spirit's baptism.

One individual may share a testimony of receiving spiritual gifts, reminiscent of the Apostle Paul's exhortation in 1 Corinthians 12:7, "To each is given the manifestation of the Spirit for the common good." These gifts may manifest as wisdom, knowledge, faith, healing, miracles, prophecy, or speaking in tongues—a vivid reminder that the Holy Spirit bestows upon believers unique tools to edify and serve the body of Christ.

Another may recount a moment when the tangible presence of the Holy Spirit enveloped them, as if echoing Jesus' promise in John 14:16-17: "And I will ask the Father, and he will give you another Helper, to be with you forever, even the Spirit of truth, whom the world cannot receive because it neither sees him nor knows him. You know him, for he dwells with you and will be in you." These encounters usher believers into a realm where the divine becomes palpable, where prayers are infused with power, and where intimacy with God is heightened.

And yet, there are those whose testimonies resonate with moments of divine empowerment, akin to the disciples who were "filled with the Holy Spirit" in Acts 2:4, enabling them to boldly proclaim the gospel. Such encounters empower believers to overcome obstacles, break through barriers, and fulfill their calling with unwavering confidence— a testament to the Holy Spirit's transformative work within.

As we navigate the narratives of diverse encounters with the Holy Spirit, we find that each story is a brushstroke in the masterpiece of God's redemptive plan. They remind us that the Spirit-filled life is not a monotonous journey but a vibrant tapestry of experiences, where the unseen force of divine power continues to shape, empower, and transform those who open their hearts to His presence.

These testimonies of diverse encounters with the Holy Spirit are like stars in the night sky, each shining with its unique brilliance and radiance. They remind us that the Holy Spirit's work is not confined to a single mold or a prescribed path but flows in dynamic and manifold ways, fulfilling the promise of Joel 2:28: "And it shall come to pass afterward, that I will pour out my Spirit on all flesh."

As we immerse ourselves in these accounts, we witness the Holy Spirit's willingness to meet us exactly where we are— whether in moments of quiet solitude or amidst the bustling chaos of life. We are reminded that the Holy Spirit's presence is not reserved for a select few but is available to all who seek Him with open hearts and hungry souls.

Furthermore, these diverse testimonies bear witness to the truth that the Holy Spirit's baptism is not a one-time event but an ongoing journey of discovery and transformation. Just as in Acts 2:38-39, Peter declared, "Repent and be baptized every one of you in the name of Jesus Christ for the forgiveness of your sins, and you will receive the gift of the Holy Spirit. For the promise is for you and for your children and for all who are far off, everyone whom the Lord our God calls to himself." The promise of the Holy Spirit's presence extends through generations, reaching us today.

In these stories, we find echoes of our own encounters, and we are encouraged to seek the Holy Spirit's guidance, empowerment, and transformative touch in our lives. The tapestry of diverse encounters with the Holy Spirit invites us to embrace the richness of our faith and to anticipate with excitement the manifold ways in which the Spirit may choose to work in and through us. As we turn the pages of these testimonies, may our hearts be stirred with expectancy, knowing that the unseen force of divine power stands ready to meet us, to empower us, and to transform us into vessels of His love and grace.

———

Diverse Encounters with the Holy Spirit

In the heart of a bustling city, Celeste, a young teacher, finds herself feeling spiritually weary. Raised in a family of faith, she knows the Holy Spirit is real, but her experiences feel distant and intellectual, more understood than felt. One evening, she attends a community prayer gathering, where believers share stories of their encounters with the Holy Spirit. Each story is different, each uniquely impactful, and Celeste listens intently, drawn in by the diversity of their experiences.

The first story comes from Skip, a soft-spoken mechanic, who describes how he felt an overwhelming sense of peace and courage when he began praying in tongues for the first time. Skip had faced anxiety about his family's future, and that moment had brought him lasting reassurance and calm. It reminds Celeste of her own moments of uncertainty and longing for stability.

Then, a woman named Amina stands up, sharing how the Spirit gave her words of wisdom in a time of crisis. Her sister had been going through a difficult divorce, and Amina, usually reserved, found herself speaking words that brought comfort and perspective. She had felt like a conduit for something greater than herself, and it strengthened her trust in the Spirit's ability to use her in ways she hadn't anticipated.

Finally, Jake, a local worship leader, describes a profound encounter he experienced while praying for someone at his church. During a service, he laid his hands on an older gentleman suffering from a long-standing illness. As he prayed, Jake felt an unexplainable warmth in his hands and a surge of faith he couldn't ignore. Within weeks, the man's condition began to improve, and the doctors couldn't explain it. Jake describes this moment as a pivotal one that deepened his confidence in the Holy Spirit's power to work through him.

As Celeste listens, she feels her own heart begin to open in a new way. She realizes the Holy Spirit's touch doesn't look the same for everyone; it moves in many ways, speaking in languages of courage, peace, wisdom, and healing. Inspired, she silently prays, "Holy Spirit, if You're this close, I want to feel You too."

That night, in the stillness of her apartment, Celeste senses a gentle presence filling her room, quieting her mind, and reminding her she is loved. It's a small but profound moment, a whisper of reassurance that she isn't alone. For the first time, the Holy Spirit feels real, personal, and near.

Celeste's experience shows that the Holy Spirit doesn't need dramatic moments to work powerfully in our lives. Sometimes, it's through the testimonies of others that we find the courage to seek our own encounters. Like Celeste, we may find that the Holy Spirit meets us uniquely, in ways that resonate with our needs and aspirations. Each story of divine touch invites us to embrace the Spirit's presence in our own lives, empowering us to live boldly, love deeply, and draw closer to God.

Transformation Through the Holy Spirit

In the grand tapestry of faith, the Holy Spirit's transformative power weaves a vibrant thread that touches lives, bringing about profound change and renewal. As we delve into this chapter, we embark on a journey of personal growth, healing, and empowerment—testimonies of lives forever altered by the presence of the Holy Spirit.

Consider the story of Mitch, whose life had been marked by addiction and despair. In the depths of his struggle, he cried out to God for deliverance, and the Holy Spirit's presence descended like a healing balm. Mitch's testimony echoes Psalm 34:17-18: "When the righteous cry for help, the Lord hears and delivers them out of all their troubles. The Lord is near to the brokenhearted and saves the crushed in spirit." Through the Holy Spirit's touch, Mitch found the strength to break free from his bondage and embark on a journey of sobriety, a testament to the transformative power of divine intervention.

Then there's Alaina, who had carried the heavy burden of unforgiveness for years. The bitterness in her heart was a stronghold that seemed insurmountable. Yet, as she yielded to the Holy Spirit's work, she experienced the truth of Ephesians 4:31-32: "Let all bitterness and wrath and anger and clamor and slander be put away from you, along with all malice. Be kind to one another, tenderhearted, forgiving one another, as God in

Christ forgave you." The Holy Spirit's presence softened her heart, enabling her to release the weight of unforgiveness and embrace a life marked by grace and reconciliation.

These testimonies of transformation are not isolated incidents but a reflection of the Holy Spirit's ongoing work within believers. Just as Paul wrote in 2 Corinthians 3:18, "And we all, with unveiled face, beholding the glory of the Lord, are being transformed into the same image from one degree of glory to another. For this comes from the Lord who is the Spirit." The Holy Spirit empowers us to shed our old selves and step into the radiant light of Christ's likeness.

Furthermore, these stories illustrate how the Holy Spirit's work leads to spiritual maturity, deepening our relationship with God and allowing us to bear the fruit of the Spirit described in Galatians 5:22-23: "But the fruit of the Spirit is love, joy, peace, patience, kindness, goodness, faithfulness, gentleness, self-control." Through the Holy Spirit's guidance, believers become vessels of God's love, radiating His character and drawing nearer to Him.

As we journey through these stories of transformation, may they serve as beacons of hope, reminding us that the Holy Spirit's baptism is not merely a ritual but a divine encounter that has the power to shatter strongholds, heal wounds, and usher us into a deeper and more profound relationship with the God who transforms lives and renews hearts.

These testimonies of transformation serve as living proof that the Holy Spirit's baptism is not a distant, historical event but a living encounter with divine power that continues to shape lives. Consider Carmen, who battled a crippling sense of worthlessness for years. Despite her achievements and successes, she felt unworthy of love and acceptance. It was only when she surrendered to the Holy Spirit's transformative touch that she understood the depth of God's love, echoing Romans 5:5: "God's love has been poured into our hearts through the Holy Spirit who has been given to us." Carmen's journey from self-doubt to self-acceptance is a testament to the Holy Spirit's profound work in healing wounded hearts.

Then there is Charles, whose life was marked by anger and hostility. His relationships were strained, and his heart was burdened with bitterness. Yet, as Charles allowed the Holy Spirit to work within him, he experienced the truth of Galatians 5:22-23: "But the fruit of the Spirit is love, joy, peace, patience, kindness, goodness, faithfulness, gentleness, self-control." The Holy Spirit's transformative power softened Charles's heart, and he learned to extend grace and forgiveness to others, mending broken relationships and finding true peace.

These stories remind us that the Holy Spirit's work is not limited by human limitations but transcends them, reaching deep into the recesses of the human heart to bring about lasting change. They demonstrate that no stronghold is too strong, no wound too deep, and no life too far gone for the Holy Spirit to transform.

As we immerse ourselves in these testimonies of personal growth, healing, and empowerment, we are invited to reflect on our own journey of transformation. We are reminded that the Holy Spirit's transformative power is available to all who seek it—a divine force that empowers us to break free from bondage, embrace God's love, and become vessels of His grace.

In the grand tapestry of faith, these stories of transformation serve as radiant threads, weaving a compelling narrative of the Holy Spirit's ongoing work within the lives of believers. They inspire us to open our hearts to the transformative touch of the Holy Spirit and to yield to His guiding hand as He leads us toward greater spiritual maturity, healing, and a deeper, more profound relationship with our Heavenly Father.

Transformation Through the Holy Spirit

Meet Judas, a man who, on the surface, seemed to have it all together. He was successful, respected in his career, and had a family who loved him. Yet beneath this exterior, he carried a weight he couldn't shake—a lingering bitterness and anger that had shaped his life for as long as he could remember. Past wounds and betrayals had hardened his heart, making him guarded and wary, and he knew that if he didn't change, his relationships and even his family would bear the brunt of his unresolved hurt.

One Sunday morning, Judas found himself in a church service, listening to stories of the Holy Spirit's power to heal and transform. Skeptical yet intrigued, he silently prayed, "If You're real, God, if this Holy Spirit is who they say He is, show me. I don't want to carry this anger anymore." In that quiet moment, he sensed a presence he couldn't quite explain, like a warmth that softened the tension in his chest. As he closed his eyes, memories of past wounds surfaced, and with them came a gentle yet powerful invitation to forgive and let go.

It didn't happen all at once, but over the following weeks, Judas found himself slowly surrendering his pain to the Holy Spirit. He was reminded of Galatians 5:22-23, the promise of the Spirit's fruit—love, joy, peace, patience, kindness, goodness, faithfulness, gentleness, and self-control. As Judas prayed, he noticed small changes. The urge to react with anger faded, replaced by a desire to respond with understanding and grace. Conversations with his family, once strained, grew lighter. His heart felt like it was healing from the inside out.

One evening, his young son approached him, saying, "Dad, you're different. I don't know what happened, but you don't get as mad anymore." This simple observation from his child cemented for Alex the reality of the Holy Spirit's transformative work. Through the Spirit's presence, he was becoming the father and husband he had always hoped to be.

Judas's story reminds us that transformation through the Holy Spirit is not just a lofty idea—it's a tangible reality that touches our lives in ways we can see and feel. Like Judas, each of us carries burdens, wounds, or patterns we long to break free from. The Holy Spirit's power is available to all who seek it, ready to bring healing, peace, and profound change. Judas's journey reveals that no heart is too hardened, no past too painful for the Spirit's gentle, transformative touch, inviting us all to open ourselves to the possibility of true renewal and freedom.

Challenges and Victories

In the realm of faith, challenges often walk hand in hand with victories, and the journey to receiving the Holy Spirit's baptism is no exception. In this section, we explore the trials and triumphs of those who faced doubt, resistance, or the need for spiritual guidance on their path toward this transformative encounter.

Meet Camille, whose heart longed for the Holy Spirit's baptism but was plagued by doubt. She questioned whether she was worthy, whether she had enough faith, echoing the plea of a father in Mark 9:24: "I believe; help my unbelief!" Camille's struggle mirrors the honest wrestling of many who grapple with uncertainty on their journey. Yet, Camille's story doesn't end with doubt. Through prayer, seeking God's Word, and the support of her faith community, she overcame her doubt and encountered the Holy Spirit's presence in a profound way—a victory that reminds us of James 1:6: "But let him ask in faith, with no doubting, for the one who doubts is like a wave of the sea that is driven and tossed by the wind."

Then there's Josiah, who faced resistance from external sources. Friends and family questioned his pursuit of the Holy Spirit's baptism, just as Jesus encountered opposition in His own ministry (Mark 3:21). Josiah's perseverance, however, serves as a beacon of hope for those who face external pressures that challenge their spiritual journey. Through steadfast faith and the guidance of his faith community, Josiah broke through the barriers of resistance and experienced the Holy Spirit's transformative touch—a victory that demonstrates the power of unity in faith.

These testimonies of challenges and victories are not unique but resonate with the shared human experience of wrestling with doubt and facing resistance. They are an invitation to those who may be on their own journey toward the Holy Spirit's baptism, providing inspiration and guidance on how to navigate the hurdles that may arise.

The stories of doubt, resistance, and eventual victory remind us that the Holy Spirit is not deterred by our uncertainties or the skepticism of others. Instead, He stands ready to meet us in our vulnerabilities, to guide us through the storms of doubt, and to lead us to the shores of victory.

As we journey through these testimonies, may they inspire and encourage all who read them, strengthening their resolve to seek the Holy Spirit's baptism and reassuring them that the unseen force of divine power is always at work, ready to break through the barriers and transform lives with the victorious touch of His presence.

These stories of challenges and victories also highlight the importance of spiritual guidance and the role of a supportive faith community. Just as Timothy received guidance and encouragement from the Apostle Paul (2 Timothy 1:6-7), individuals facing doubt or resistance often find solace and wisdom through the counsel of mentors, pastors, or fellow believers who have walked similar paths. This guidance serves as a beacon of hope, guiding seekers toward a deeper understanding of the Holy Spirit's work and His desire to empower and transform lives.

Moreover, these testimonies remind us of the truth found in Romans 8:31: "What then shall we say to these things? If God is for us, who can be against us?" Despite the challenges and opposition faced on the journey to receiving the Holy Spirit's baptism, the ultimate victory belongs to God. These stories bear witness to the unfailing faithfulness of the One who promises in Isaiah 41:10, "Fear not, for I am with you; be not dismayed, for I am your God; I will strengthen you, I will help you, I will uphold you with my righteous right hand."

In the end, the challenges encountered on the path to receiving the Holy Spirit's baptism become stepping stones to victory, testifying to the transformative power of faith, perseverance, and reliance on God's guidance. As we absorb these testimonies, may they inspire all seekers to press on in their own journeys, knowing that the challenges they face can be overcome by the unwavering love and power of the Holy Spirit, who stands ready to grant the victorious experience of His presence and empowerment.

———

Challenges and Victories on the Path to the Holy Spirit's Baptism

Meet Joshua, a quiet, thoughtful man in his mid-thirties, who'd spent years in his faith community but had always felt something was missing—a deeper connection, a sense of empowerment. He often heard others speak of the Holy Spirit's baptism, but doubt shadowed his desire. "Is this truly for me?" he wondered. "Am I worthy of such an experience?" Like many, Joshua struggled with self-doubt, echoing the words of Mark 9:24, "I believe; help my unbelief!"

Joshua tried to push the feeling aside, but his longing grew stronger. Seeking answers, he turned to his pastor, who encouraged him to pray, study the Word, and trust that God's promises were meant for him too. Yet, his doubts remained, and in his quiet moments, he felt like he was staring at a wall he couldn't climb.

Then, Joshua confided in his close friends from church. They reminded him of God's words in James 1:6: "But let him ask in faith, with no doubting." Together, they prayed, and slowly, Joshua's fear started to fade. As he let go of his self-doubt, he began to feel a stirring inside, a warmth that grew with each step of faith. Finally, one evening in a simple prayer gathering, he felt the Holy Spirit's presence wash over him. The peace, joy, and strength he'd longed for filled him, transforming his faith in a way he'd never known.

Joshua's journey was not without opposition. Some family members doubted and questioned his pursuit, wondering why he felt the need for "more." Yet, like David in Scripture, Joshua persevered. His faith community became his anchor, and through their support and his deepening trust in God, he broke through the barriers of resistance.

Today, Joshua's testimony resonates with those who doubt or face external pressures on their spiritual journey. His story shows that despite challenges, the Holy Spirit stands ready to meet us in our doubts and fears. Joshua's victory over his doubts became a testimony of God's faithfulness and the power of perseverance.

His journey reminds us all that the Holy Spirit's baptism is not reserved for those without doubts or struggles. The Spirit works with us as we are, meeting us in our uncertainties and leading us to a place of victory. Joshua's story is a beacon for anyone feeling unworthy, unsure, or facing resistance, showing that God's promises are steadfast and that the Spirit is always ready to empower, transform, and bring victory to those who seek Him.

―――――

Conclusion

In closing the chapter titled "The Flame Within: Personal Testimonies of the Holy Spirit's Baptism," we find ourselves standing on sacred ground, surrounded by the echoes of faith, the power of transformation, and the undeniable presence of the Holy Spirit. These testimonies have been our guides on a journey through the depths of personal encounters with the divine—the kind of encounters that leave us forever changed.

As we've walked alongside individuals who have felt the warmth of the Holy Spirit's embrace, witnessed the miraculous outpouring of spiritual gifts, and experienced the profound transformation of their hearts, we've seen that the Spirit-filled life is not a mere concept but a living reality. These testimonies bear witness to the truth that the Holy Spirit is not confined to ancient history but is active and alive in the lives of believers today.

These stories are not isolated incidents, but they collectively proclaim the enduring promise of Acts 2:38-39: "Repent and be baptized every one of you in the name of Jesus Christ for the forgiveness of your sins, and you will receive the gift of the Holy Spirit. For the promise is for you and for your children and for all who are far off, everyone whom the Lord our God calls to himself." This promise, made millennia ago, continues to resound in the lives of those who earnestly seek the Holy Spirit's presence.

As we draw this chapter to a close, let us carry these testimonies with us, like a torch that lights the path of our own faith journey. May they serve as reminders that the Holy Spirit's baptism is not a distant dream but a living, breathing reality that awaits those who open their hearts in earnest pursuit of His presence. The flame within, ignited by the Holy Spirit, burns brightly, offering us guidance, comfort, empowerment, and transformation.

The testimonies we've encountered in this chapter are not merely stories; they are testimonies to the ongoing, life-changing work of the Holy Spirit. They are an invitation, a promise, and a proclamation that the Spirit-filled life is within reach for all who call upon the name of the Lord. As we continue our journey, may our hearts remain open to the unseen force of divine power, the Holy Spirit, who longs to fill us, transform us, and set our hearts ablaze with His presence.

CHAPTER SEVEN

Signs of Fire: Instances of Divine Presence in Scripture and Modern Times

"By day the Lord went ahead of them in a pillar of cloud to guide them on their way and by night in a pillar of fire to give them light, so that they could travel by day or night." — EXODUS 13:21 NIV

Welcome, dear reader, to Chapter 7 of "Spirit Filled Life: The Unseen Force of Divine Power." In this captivating chapter titled "Signs of Fire: Instances of Divine Presence in Scripture and Modern Times," we embark on a remarkable journey that spans the pages of the Bible and extends into the narratives of contemporary life. It is a chapter where the ordinary meets the extraordinary, where the natural world intersects with the supernatural realm, and where we delve deep into the purpose and significance of signs of fire and miraculous manifestations.

As we turn the pages of this chapter, we will find ourselves immersed in the sacred texts of old, encountering profound moments when the presence of God was tangibly manifested through signs of fire. We will witness the awe-inspiring accounts of a burning bush that caught the attention of Moses, the pillar of fire that guided the Israelites through the wilderness, and the fiery chariot that bore Elijah into the heavens. These ancient stories are not mere historical artifacts but living testimonies to the power and presence of the Holy Spirit.

But our journey does not end in the distant past. We will also delve into the narratives of our modern times, where signs and wonders continue to unfold in the lives of believers. These contemporary accounts are a testament to the fact that the Holy Spirit's role is as vibrant and relevant today as it was in ages past. They affirm the enduring truth of God's Word, confirm the gospel message, and point us to the glory of God.

Prepare to be captivated by stories of healing, divine intervention, and supernatural encounters that leave us in awe of the Holy Spirit's enduring presence and power.

Yet, as we explore these miraculous manifestations, we will also emphasize the importance of a balanced perspective.

While signs and wonders are awe-inspiring, they are not the ultimate goal of our faith.

They are signposts that point us toward the glorious destination—intimate communion with God. These manifestations are invitations to draw nearer to the One who is the source of all power, grounded in His unchanging Word, and centered on His glory.

So, dear reader, as you embark on this journey through Chapter 7, prepare to be inspired, challenged, and encouraged. May your understanding of the Holy Spirit's role in your life deepen, and may you walk away with a renewed sense of awe and wonder at the unseen force of divine power that is at work within you and among us all.

Biblical Manifestations of Divine Presence

In the pages of the Bible, we encounter awe-inspiring moments when the presence of God blazed like fire, leaving an indelible mark on the hearts and minds of those who witnessed these divine manifestations. One such moment transports us back to the arid terrain of Sinai, where Moses, the humble shepherd turned reluctant leader, found himself before a bush that burned but was not consumed. It was a breathtaking sight—a fire that flickered with a divine message. In Exodus 3:2, we read: "And the angel of the Lord appeared to him in a flame of fire out of the midst of a bush. He looked, and behold, the bush was burning, yet it was not consumed." This fiery spectacle was a profound encounter with the presence of God

Himself. It was an invitation to draw near, to remove his sandals and stand on holy ground, for the Creator of the universe was there, speaking His name, "I AM WHO I AM." This was not merely a fire; it was the radiant manifestation of the living God, a foreshadowing of the Holy Spirit's presence that would come to dwell within believers.

Another remarkable manifestation of divine presence through fire unfolded as the Israelites embarked on their journey through the wilderness. During the day, they were led by a pillar of cloud, but as night descended, a pillar of fire blazed forth to guide them. In Exodus 13:21-22, we read: "And the Lord went before them by day in a pillar of cloud to lead them along the way, and by night in a pillar of fire to give them light, that they might travel by day and by night." This fiery pillar was more than a celestial compass; it was the reassuring presence of God, a beacon of hope and guidance for a people journeying toward the Promised Land. Just as the Israelites followed this divine fire, believers today are led by the Holy Spirit, illuminating the path of righteousness and truth.

The story of Elijah, the fiery prophet, offers yet another glimpse into the manifestations of divine presence through fire. In 2 Kings 2:11, we witness the extraordinary moment when "behold, chariots of fire and horses of fire separated the two of them [Elijah and Elisha]. And Elijah went up by a whirlwind into heaven." This fiery chariot that bore Elijah into the heavens was not merely a mode of transportation; it was a supernatural sign that marked his departure from earthly life.

It testified to the power and authority of the God of Israel, whose presence was not confined to earthly realms. Just as Elijah's chariot of fire defied the laws of nature, the Holy Spirit's presence in believers defies human understanding, empowering them to transcend the limitations of the natural world.

These biblical manifestations of divine presence through fire were not mere pyrotechnic displays; they were profound encounters with the living God. The burning bush, the pillar of fire, and the fiery chariot were all tangible reminders that the Holy Spirit's presence has always been at the center of God's relationship with humanity. Just as fire both consumes and refines, these divine manifestations remind us that the Holy Spirit purifies, guides, and empowers those who seek Him.

In contemplating these biblical manifestations of divine presence through fire, we are drawn into a profound understanding of the Holy Spirit's role in the lives of believers. Just as the burning bush, the pillar of fire, and the fiery chariot served as tangible signs of God's presence in the Old Testament, the Holy Spirit's presence today is a living reality in the lives of those who have received Him.

The burning bush reminds us that the Holy Spirit is not a distant, impersonal force but a living and approachable God who calls us to draw near. Just as Moses removed his sandals in reverence for the holy ground, we too are invited to approach the presence of God with humility and awe. The

Holy Spirit beckons us to enter into a relationship with the living God, where we can hear His voice and know His name.

The pillar of fire that guided the Israelites through the wilderness speaks to the Holy Spirit's role as our constant guide and source of illumination. In our spiritual journey, we may find ourselves in the dark, uncertain moments of life. Yet, just as the pillar of fire provided light and direction, the Holy Spirit is our guiding light, leading us through life's challenges and uncertainties. He brings clarity to our path and assures us that we are not alone.

Elijah's fiery chariot reminds us that the Holy Spirit empowers us to transcend the limitations of this world. Just as Elijah was taken up in a whirlwind, believers are empowered by the Holy Spirit to go beyond the ordinary, to walk in the supernatural, and to fulfill the divine calling on their lives. The Holy Spirit equips us with gifts and abilities that go beyond our natural talents, enabling us to carry out God's purposes in extraordinary ways.

As we reflect on these biblical manifestations, we are reminded that the Holy Spirit's presence is not confined to the pages of Scripture but is a living reality in the lives of believers today. Just as fire refines and purifies, the Holy Spirit works in our hearts, transforming us into vessels that bear His presence and reflect His glory. These manifestations of divine presence through fire serve as enduring symbols of the Holy Spirit's ongoing work, inviting us to experience the reality of His presence in our own lives.

Encountering the Divine Fire
of the Holy Spirit

Meet Sam, a man in his late forties, who had spent years feeling lost in the wilderness of life's struggles. Working long hours in a high-stress job, he'd started to feel a deep emptiness inside. Though he attended church and read the Bible, he struggled to experience God's presence. He longed for more but wasn't sure what was missing. He often thought of Moses at the burning bush—a place where God's presence was undeniable and transforming. Sam wondered if he'd ever feel that closeness himself.

Then, one Sunday, Sam heard a sermon about God's divine manifestations through fire—the bush that burned without being consumed, the pillar of fire that led the Israelites, and the fiery chariot that carried Elijah to heaven. It stirred something within him. Inspired, he went home and prayed, "God, I don't need to see fire, but I need to feel Your presence. Guide me like You guided them."

The next morning, as he prayed quietly, he sensed a warmth deep in his spirit, like a gentle flame. For the first time, Sam felt God's nearness, and it filled him with peace he'd never known. His prayer life changed as he felt the Holy Spirit's presence guiding him like that ancient pillar of fire, illuminating his thoughts and giving him a new sense of direction. In moments of doubt or fear, he found comfort in knowing the Holy Spirit was walking beside him.

Over time, Sam's life transformed. The empty feelings disappeared, replaced by a renewed energy and purpose, as if the Holy Spirit were refining and strengthening him. Just as fire both illuminates and purifies, Sam realized the Spirit was doing the same within him, burning away old anxieties and replacing them with a steady confidence in God's presence.

Sam's journey reminds us that the Holy Spirit's guidance and refining power are as present today as they were in the Bible. His story calls us to seek that divine fire for ourselves, inviting the Holy Spirit to lead, comfort, and transform us. It's a reminder that the same Spirit who spoke to Moses, led the Israelites, and empowered Elijah is alive in our lives, ready to guide and refine us through the challenges of our daily walk.

Modern Miracles and Divine Encounters

The ripple effect of baptism extends far beyond the moment when water touches skin and soul. It is a transformation not meant to be solitary but communal, an invitation to become a vital part of the faith family. In the immediate aftermath of baptism, individuals often find themselves at the threshold of a new spiritual home—a community of believers ready to embrace them, nurture their faith, and walk alongside them in their journey.

In the tapestry of modern life, threads of the extraordinary are often woven among the ordinary, testifying to the timeless presence and power of the Holy Spirit. As we explore contemporary stories of miraculous encounters with signs of fire and divine manifestations, we find that the extraordinary is not confined to the pages of ancient scrolls but is an ever-present reality for those who open their hearts to the Holy Spirit's work.

Consider the remarkable story of Brielle, a young woman who had struggled with a debilitating illness for years. Her days were marked by pain and limitations, until one fateful evening when she attended a prayer gathering. As the prayers of believers rose like incense, Brielle suddenly felt an intense warmth enveloping her. It was as if a fire had ignited within her very being, and in that moment, her pain dissolved. The doctors were astounded, unable to explain her sudden and complete healing. Brielle's experience echoes the words of Psalm 103:3, "who forgives all your iniquity, who heals all your diseases." Her healing was not just a medical marvel; it was a divine encounter that bore witness to the Holy Spirit's healing touch.

In another account, Philip, a man of unwavering faith, found himself in a dire financial crisis. With mounting debts and no apparent way out, he turned to prayer and fasting. One night, as he fervently sought God's guidance, a supernatural sign appeared. In his small room, a gentle fire-like glow emanated from a simple painting of Jesus on the wall. As he gazed upon it, a deep peace settled in his heart, and an idea emerged that would lead to a breakthrough in his financial situation. Philip's encounter resonates with the promise of Philippians 4:19, "And my God will supply every need of yours according to his riches in glory in Christ Jesus." It was a modern-day manifestation of divine provision through a sign of fire.

These modern-day encounters with divine presence and manifestations align with biblical accounts of God's miraculous work in the lives of His people. Just as the Israelites witnessed the pillar of fire guiding them through the wilderness, and Elijah ascended in a fiery chariot, contemporary believers encounter signs of fire that illuminate their paths and bring breakthroughs in their lives. These stories reaffirm the Holy Spirit's role as the Comforter, the Healer, the Provider, and the One who works miracles in our midst.

These are not isolated incidents but a chorus of testimonies, echoing the words of Jesus in John 14:12, "Truly, truly, I say to you, whoever believes in me will also do the works that I do; and greater works than these will he do because I am going to the Father." They invite us to embrace the reality of the Holy Spirit's presence in our lives, reminding us that signs of fire and divine manifestations are not relics of the past but living testimonies of His enduring work among us.

One cannot help but recall the words of Acts 2:17-18, where the apostle Peter proclaimed, "And in the last days, it shall be, God declares, that I will pour out my Spirit on all flesh, and your sons and your daughters shall prophesy, and your young men shall see visions, and your old men shall dream dreams; even on my male servants and female servants in those days I will pour out my Spirit, and they shall prophesy." These contemporary encounters are a testament to the fulfillment of this promise.

Consider the story of April, a woman who had faced years of emotional and spiritual turmoil. Her heart longed for a deeper connection with God, and one day, as she poured out her soul in prayer, a radiant light suddenly filled her room. It danced and flickered like a celestial flame, and April felt an overwhelming sense of peace and love wash over her. It was as if the Holy Spirit was enveloping her in His embrace, dispelling the darkness that had clouded her heart. Her encounter mirrors the words of Psalm 36:9, "For with you is the fountain of life; in your light do we see light." April's experience reminds us that the Holy Spirit is not distant but ever-present, ready to illuminate our lives with His light.

These modern manifestations of divine presence are not limited to personal encounters alone. Consider the gathering of believers in a small church where, during a time of worship, a brilliant fire-like glow appeared above the congregation. It hovered like a radiant cloud, and the atmosphere was charged with an overwhelming sense of God's presence.

Many wept tears of joy, and others were filled with a deep sense of awe and reverence. It was as if the Holy Spirit had descended in a tangible way, reminding them of Acts 2:3, where "tongues as of fire appeared to them and rested on each one of them." This divine manifestation left an indelible mark on the hearts of those who witnessed it, reinforcing their faith in the living God.

These contemporary stories of miraculous encounters and divine manifestations are not mere anomalies but profound testimonies to the ongoing work of the Holy Spirit in our lives. They echo the words of Hebrews 13:8, "Jesus Christ is the same yesterday and today and forever," reminding us that the God of the burning bush, the pillar of fire, and the fiery chariot is still active and present in our lives today. These stories invite us to embrace the reality of the Holy Spirit's power, prompting us to seek His presence and anticipate the extraordinary in our own journeys of faith. Just as the Israelites followed the pillar of fire, and Elijah witnessed the fiery chariot, contemporary believers are called to follow the leading of the Holy Spirit's manifestations, trusting in His guidance, provision, healing, and comfort.

A Modern Encounter with the Divine Flame

Nathanael stood on the shores of transformation, his clothes still dripping from the baptismal waters. His heart, freshly washed by the act of baptism, felt lighter, and the sense of being part of something greater than himself was overwhelming. For years, Nathanael had wandered through life without a spiritual anchor, his days filled with routine and his relationships superficial at best. But this day marked a new beginning.

Nathanael had always believed in God, but his faith felt quiet, reserved. He prayed, he attended church, but his spiritual life seemed distant from the extraordinary stories he read in the Bible. Could the miracles of fire and light he saw in the pages of Scripture still exist today? He'd never seen anything like it.

Then, during a particularly trying season—marked by an unexpected job loss and growing financial strain—Nathanael found himself yearning for a sense of assurance. One evening, as he sat in his living room, he cried out in prayer. With heartfelt desperation, he asked God for a sign, a clear direction for his future.

Suddenly, he felt a warmth in the room. He opened his eyes and, to his amazement, noticed a soft glow coming from a painting of Jesus on the wall. The light was gentle, almost like a flame, illuminating the room with a warmth that seemed otherworldly. It felt as if the Holy Spirit had entered his space, filling him with a profound sense of peace and comfort. In that instant, Nathanael knew he wasn't alone; he sensed God's presence, His assurance that everything would be alright.

That experience transformed him. Nathanael found renewed faith, a confidence he hadn't felt before. He took proactive steps toward a new career, each one guided by that peace he had felt in the room that night. Just as the Israelites were guided by the pillar of fire, Nathanael felt the Holy Spirit guiding him, step by step, on his own path. This modern encounter with divine presence became the bedrock of Nathanael's life, deepening his faith and instilling in him a hope he had never known before.

Nathanael's story reminds us that the Holy Spirit is ever-present and active, that moments of divine manifestation still happen today. His experience calls us to believe that the God of fire, light, and miracles continues to reveal Himself to those who seek Him, inviting us to trust in His guidance and open ourselves to encounters that strengthen our faith in the journey ahead.

———

Theology of Divine Signs and Wonders

As we embark on a theological exploration of signs of fire and miraculous manifestations, we enter a realm where the natural meets the supernatural, where the temporal intersects with the eternal. It is a journey that beckons us to unravel the purpose and significance of these signs, both in the sacred texts of old and in the narratives of our modern lives. At its core, this exploration is a pursuit of understanding how these signs align with the teachings of the Bible regarding the Holy Spirit's role in the life of believers, in confirming the gospel message, and in pointing to the glory of God.

When we peer into the pages of the Bible, we encounter a tapestry of signs and wonders that serve as signposts on the path of faith. From the parting of the Red Sea to the raising of the dead, these miracles bear witness to the supernatural power of God. In the New Testament, we witness the outpouring of the Holy Spirit on the Day of Pentecost, marked by tongues of fire resting on believers' heads (Acts 2:3). This supernatural occurrence was not a mere spectacle but a divine confirmation of the fulfillment of Christ's promise to send the Holy Spirit (Acts 1:5). It signaled the birth of the Church and the empowerment of believers for the mission of spreading the gospel to the ends of the earth.

In the modern context, signs and wonders continue to unfold, reminding us that the Holy Spirit's role has not waned but is as vibrant as ever. These manifestations confirm the enduring truth of God's Word and the gospel message. They serve as beacons of hope in a world often shrouded in darkness, pointing us to the reality of God's presence and power. Just as the Apostle Paul wrote in 1 Corinthians 2:4, "My message and my preaching were not with wise and persuasive words, but with a demonstration of the Spirit's power," signs and wonders today accompany the proclamation of the gospel, testifying to its life-transforming efficacy.

Yet, it is essential to approach signs and wonders with a balanced perspective. While they are awe-inspiring and faith-building, they are not an end in themselves. They are meant to direct our gaze toward the ultimate source of power and glory—God Himself. Signs of fire and miraculous manifestations are not substitutes for faith but catalysts that propel us into deeper relationship with the Triune God. As we navigate this theological landscape, we are reminded of the words of Jesus in John 14:12, "Truly, truly, I say to you, whoever believes in me will also do the works that I do; and greater works than these will he do." It is an invitation to walk in the miraculous, anchored in the unchanging truths of Scripture, and centered on the glory of God.

In conclusion, our exploration of signs of fire and divine manifestations is a journey that traverses the boundaries of time and space, bridging the gap between the ancient and the modern. It is a testimony to the Holy Spirit's enduring presence and power, confirming the unshakable truths of Scripture and pointing us toward the glory of God. These signs remind us that we serve a God who is both the author of creation and the orchestrator of miracles, inviting us to walk in the extraordinary while rooted in the eternal.

As we conclude our theological exploration of signs of fire and miraculous manifestations, we find ourselves at the intersection of faith and the supernatural. It is a place where the ancient and the contemporary converge, where the sacred Scriptures resonate with the stories of our lives today. In this journey, we have uncovered the purpose and significance of these signs, guided by the timeless teachings of the Bible and the ongoing work of the Holy Spirit.

Throughout our exploration, we have seen that signs and wonders serve as divinely appointed markers on the path of faith. They are not arbitrary displays of power but intentional manifestations that affirm the truth of God's Word. Just as the pillar of fire guided the Israelites through the wilderness and the tongues of fire marked the birth of the Church, contemporary signs of fire and miraculous encounters confirm the gospel message and the ongoing presence of the Holy Spirit in the lives of believers.

At the same time, we have emphasized the importance of a balanced perspective. Signs and wonders, while awe-inspiring, are not the ultimate goal of our faith. They are the signposts that point us toward the glorious destination— intimate communion with God. These manifestations are invitations to draw nearer to the One who is the source of all power and the author of our faith. They prompt us to seek a deeper relationship with the Triune God, grounded in His unchanging Word and centered on His glory.

In the words of the Apostle Paul in 1 Corinthians 12:7, "Now to each one the manifestation of the Spirit is given for the common good." Signs of fire and miraculous encounters are not meant for personal validation but for the edification of the body of Christ and the proclamation of the gospel. They are a reminder that the Holy Spirit empowers us to carry out the mission of sharing the good news with a world in need of hope and transformation.

As we step away from this theological exploration, may we carry with us a deepened understanding of the Holy Spirit's role in our lives. May we walk in the confidence that signs and wonders are not relics of the past but an ongoing reality, affirming our faith and leading us to a deeper encounter with God. May we embrace the balance of awe and humility, recognizing that the greatest miracle of all is the redemptive work of Christ in our hearts. And may our lives bear witness to the reality that the unseen force of divine power, the Holy Spirit, is at work within us and among us, guiding us toward a future filled with hope and glory.

———————

Encountering the Miraculous in Modern Faith

Alyssa had always felt a quiet, steady faith in God. She grew up hearing the stories of biblical miracles, like the parting of the Red Sea and the flames of Pentecost, but they felt like something distant, confined to the pages of history. Could such miraculous signs still happen today? She wasn't so sure.

Then, during a difficult season in her life, Alyssa's faith was tested. She was going through a painful health crisis, and each day felt like a struggle. One evening, after weeks of feeling helpless, she attended a prayer service with her church community. The sanctuary was peaceful, the lights dimmed, as voices lifted in prayer and worship. Alyssa closed her eyes and quietly prayed, asking God for a sign of hope, anything to let her know He was near.

As she prayed, a warmth began to fill the room, a tangible presence that was impossible to ignore. When she opened her eyes, she noticed a faint glow at the front of the sanctuary, like a soft, ethereal flame hovering above the altar. It felt surreal. A sense of peace washed over her, a peace that went beyond understanding. In that moment, Alyssa felt something shift within her—a deep-seated assurance that God was present, working even in her struggles. She knew without a doubt that she wasn't alone, and that the Holy Spirit was with her, guiding her forward.

From that day, Alyssa's outlook changed. Her struggles didn't vanish overnight, but her faith grew stronger. This small, divine sign became an anchor for her, reminding her of God's unshakable presence. She shared her story with others, and her experience became a beacon of hope for those going through their own challenges. The glow she witnessed, though subtle, had lit up her faith and deepened her relationship with God in ways she hadn't imagined.

Alyssa's story reminds us that signs and wonders, even in their simplest form, are more than just divine displays; they're intimate invitations to trust in God's presence in our lives. They remind us that the Holy Spirit's power is not just a thing of the past but a living reality, meeting us in our present with gentle strength. For Alyssa, and for all who seek God, such encounters offer hope, drawing us closer to the One who has promised never to leave us.

———

Conclusion

In closing this captivating chapter, we find ourselves at the crossroads of faith and the miraculous, where the sacred and the contemporary intertwine to reveal the profound nature of divine presence. Our journey through "Signs of Fire: Instances of Divine Presence in Scripture and Modern Times" has taken us from the burning bush that caught the attention of Moses to the awe-inspiring accounts of contemporary believers who have witnessed signs and wonders in their own lives. It is a journey that reminds us of the enduring power and presence of the Holy Spirit.

As we reflect on the purpose and significance of signs of fire and miraculous manifestations, we are reminded that these phenomena are not mere spectacles but powerful confirmations of God's Word and His ongoing work in the world. From the pillar of fire that guided the Israelites through the wilderness to the fiery chariot that carried Elijah into the heavens, these ancient stories bear witness to the Holy Spirit's enduring role in empowering believers and confirming the gospel message.

In our modern era, we have encountered stories of healing, divine intervention, and supernatural encounters that continue to affirm the Holy Spirit's presence and power. These contemporary accounts serve as beacons of hope in a world often shrouded in darkness, pointing us to the reality of God's presence and His unwavering commitment to His people. They remind us that the Holy Spirit's role is not confined to history but is as vibrant and relevant as ever.

Yet, as we embrace these miraculous manifestations, we are also called to maintain a balanced perspective. Signs and wonders, while awe-inspiring, are not the ultimate goal of our faith. They are signposts that lead us to a deeper relationship with the Triune God, grounded in His unchanging Word and centered on His glory. These manifestations prompt us to draw nearer to the One who is the source of all power and the author of our faith.

So, dear reader, as we conclude this chapter, may you carry with you a deeper understanding of the Holy Spirit's role in your life. May you walk in the confidence that signs and wonders are not relics of the past but an ongoing reality, affirming your faith and leading you to a more profound encounter with God. May you embrace the balance of awe and humility, recognizing that the greatest miracle of all is the redemptive work of Christ in your heart. And may your life bear witness to the reality that the unseen force of divine power, the Holy Spirit, is at work within you and among us, guiding us toward a future filled with hope and glory.

CHAPTER EIGHT

A Life Transformed: The Tenfold Impact of Embracing the Holy Spirit

"Therefore, if anyone is in Christ, the new creation has come: The old has gone, the new is here!" — 2 CORINTHIANS 5:17 NIV

Welcome to the awe-inspiring journey that awaits in Chapter 8, where we delve deep into the profound impact of embracing the Holy Spirit—a journey that promises to transform every dimension of our lives. Titled "A Life Transformed: The Tenfold Impact of Embracing the Holy Spirit," this chapter unfolds as an intricately woven tapestry of spiritual awakening, personal renewal, and the blossoming of extraordinary gifts. As we step into this sacred exploration, we find ourselves in the midst of a divine encounter that empowers, rejuvenates, and redefines our very existence.

In the realm of embracing the Holy Spirit, we encounter a wellspring of transformative power. It is a power that equips individuals to surmount challenges that once seemed insurmountable. Through a treasury of real-life stories and practical examples, we witness how embracing the Holy Spirit provides believers with an unwavering strength—a strength that enables them to rise above adversity, break free from the shackles of despair, and embark on a journey of spiritual growth.

But the impact does not end there; it unfolds like the petals of a blossoming flower, revealing the divine fragrance of spiritual fruit. As we meander through the intricate landscape of love, joy, peace, patience, kindness, goodness, faithfulness, gentleness, and self-control—the fruits of the Spirit—we are enchanted by the depth of character transformation they bring. Through stories and anecdotes that resonate with authenticity, we witness how these virtues become an integral part of believers' lives, radiating warmth, harmony, and a sense of purpose.

Yet, the transformation does not cease with character alone. It extends its embrace to the realm of spiritual gifts. We unravel stories of prophecy, healing, speaking in tongues, and the awe-inspiring miracles that unfold when individuals embrace the Holy Spirit fully. These gifts are not relics of a bygone era but living expressions of the Spirit's continuous work, enriching the lives of believers and igniting their ministries with divine power.

As we embark on this transformative odyssey, we are reminded that embracing the Holy Spirit is not a passive endeavor but an active partnership with the divine. It is an invitation to a life that transcends the ordinary, where the impact of the Spirit knows no bounds, and where lives are forever changed. Through these pages, we explore the profound tenfold impact of embracing the Holy Spirit—a journey that redefines our understanding of faith, love, and the limitless potential that awaits when we welcome the Spirit into every corner of our lives. So, dear reader, fasten your seatbelts, for we are about to embark on an extraordinary voyage of discovery and transformation.

The Transformative Power of the Holy Spirit

In Chapter 8, Topic 1, we embark on a journey that delves into the extraordinary realm of transformation, one that is ignited and sustained by the profound presence of the Holy Spirit. It is here, within the embrace of the Holy Spirit, that believers experience a depth of change that transcends the ordinary and ushers them into the extraordinary. This transformation isn't limited to mere superficial alterations; rather, it is a profound metamorphosis that touches every aspect of their lives.

The Holy Spirit, often referred to as the "unseen force of divine power," takes center stage as we explore its capacity to empower believers in their journey of faith. It equips them with the strength, resilience, and guidance needed to overcome life's challenges, both internal and external. Through the empowering work of the Holy Spirit, individuals discover the ability to break free from the strongholds that have held them captive for far too long. These may include addictions, destructive thought patterns, or past traumas that have hindered personal growth and well-being.

To illustrate the transformative power of the Holy Spirit, we turn to real-life testimonies that showcase the remarkable stories of individuals who have embraced this divine force in their lives. These personal accounts serve as living proof of the Holy Spirit's ability to foster spiritual maturity, guiding individuals on a path toward a deeper relationship with the divine. Through the Holy Spirit's intervention, emotional healing becomes more than just a distant dream—it becomes a tangible reality, as individuals find solace and restoration in the presence of the Comforter.

Furthermore, the Holy Spirit equips believers with the resilience needed to navigate life's adversities. As we journey through biblical examples and contemporary stories, we discover that the Holy Spirit provides not only the strength to endure trials but also the wisdom to learn from them. It is through these challenges that believers experience a renewed sense of purpose and a heightened awareness of the Holy Spirit's transformative work in their lives.

In this exploration, we find that the transformative power of the Holy Spirit is not confined to one aspect of life; rather, it extends its influence into every corner of our existence. From spiritual maturity and emotional healing to the capacity to overcome adversity, the Holy Spirit's transformative touch is an awe-inspiring force that invites believers to embrace the fullness of their faith journey. Through the guidance of Scripture and the real-life experiences of those who have walked this path, we are reminded of the enduring and life-altering impact of the Holy Spirit's presence.

As we journey deeper into the transformative power of the Holy Spirit, we uncover the profound stories and scriptural insights that illustrate its impact on believers' lives. Let us turn our gaze to the pages of the Bible, where the Holy Spirit's transformative work has been evident for centuries.

One of the most striking examples of the Holy Spirit's transformative power can be found in the life of the Apostle Paul. In his early years, Paul was known as Saul, a zealous persecutor of Christians. However, a dramatic encounter with the risen Christ on the road to Damascus, empowered and guided by the Holy Spirit, transformed him into one of the most influential figures in early Christianity. His story serves as a powerful testament to the Holy Spirit's ability to radically change hearts and redirect life's course.

Throughout the New Testament, we encounter accounts of individuals who, through the indwelling of the Holy Spirit, experienced personal growth and renewal. The once-fearful disciples, who cowered in the upper room after Christ's crucifixion, were transformed into bold and fearless evangelists after receiving the Holy Spirit at Pentecost. Their lives were marked by a newfound spiritual maturity that empowered them to spread the gospel message throughout the world.

Emotional healing, another facet of the Holy Spirit's transformative power, can be seen in the life of the woman at the well in Samaria. Her encounter with Jesus, driven by the Holy Spirit's divine appointment, led to the healing of her broken heart and the restoration of her soul. This transformation not only impacted her but also inspired an entire community to turn to Christ.

The Holy Spirit's role in overcoming adversity is vividly portrayed in the life of Joseph in the Old Testament. Despite facing betrayal, slavery, and imprisonment, Joseph's unwavering faith and reliance on the Spirit's guidance ultimately led to his exaltation and the rescue of his family from famine. His story serves as a timeless example of the Holy Spirit's capacity to enable believers to rise above life's challenges.

In the modern context, we encounter numerous testimonies of individuals whose lives have been transformed by the Holy Spirit's empowering presence. These stories stand as living proof that the Holy Spirit's transformative work is not confined to the pages of Scripture but continues to be a vibrant and life-altering force in the lives of believers today.

As we journey through this section, we will explore these stories, reflecting on the biblical examples and contemporary testimonies that showcase the remarkable transformation brought about by embracing the Holy Spirit. It is a journey that invites us to open our hearts and minds to the limitless possibilities of growth, healing, and resilience that the Holy Spirit offers to all who embrace its transformative power.

The Transformative Power of the Holy Spirit

In the midst of life's trials, Bianca found herself at a crossroads. Struggling with an overwhelming sense of worthlessness and feeling trapped by the past, she yearned for something that could bring her a sense of peace and purpose. She tried everything to break free from her anxiety and self-doubt, but nothing seemed to fill the void.

One evening, while attending a small group study on the Holy Spirit, Bianca was moved by the story of the Apostle Paul. His transformation from Saul, a fierce persecutor of Christians, to Paul, a devoted follower of Christ, struck a chord in her. She couldn't ignore the hope it stirred within her—if someone like Saul could change so radically, perhaps there was hope for her, too.

Encouraged, Bianca opened herself up in prayer, asking for the Holy Spirit to work in her life. In that quiet, vulnerable moment, she felt a gentle yet profound presence, like a light pouring into her heart. It was as if the weight of her past melted away, replaced by a peace she had never experienced. She felt the Holy Spirit's assurance that she was not only loved but also worthy, forgiven, and capable of a new beginning.

In the weeks that followed, Bianca noticed a change in herself. Old habits of self-criticism began to fade, replaced by a newfound sense of confidence and calm. She found herself drawn to Scripture, and her relationships deepened as she began sharing her journey of faith with others. For Bianca, the Holy Spirit became a source of comfort and strength, helping her overcome the doubts and emotional scars she had carried for so long.

Bianca's story shows us that the transformative power of the Holy Spirit isn't just a lesson in theology; it's a life-changing reality. For anyone struggling to find healing or a fresh start, Bianca's experience reveals that the Holy Spirit's touch can bring true freedom and a renewed sense of purpose. Her story is a reminder that when we invite the Holy Spirit into our lives, we open ourselves to a divine force that doesn't merely lift us up temporarily but walks with us, sustaining and guiding us through every step of our journey.

―――――――

Walking in Spiritual Gifts

Within the embrace of the Holy Spirit, believers uncover a treasure trove of spiritual gifts, each endowed with unique capabilities and profound purposes. In this section, we embark on a journey to explore these divine gifts mentioned in the New Testament, gifts such as prophecy, healing, and speaking in tongues. These gifts are not merely abstract concepts but are living expressions of the Holy Spirit's presence and empowerment in the lives of believers.

The gift of prophecy, as articulated in 1 Corinthians 12:10, is a powerful channel through which believers receive and communicate divine revelations and messages. It is a gift that transcends the boundaries of time and space, offering insights and guidance that can illuminate the path of faith. As we navigate the stories of those who have embraced this gift, we encounter individuals whose lives have been profoundly impacted by the prophetic word, guiding them through the twists and turns of life's journey.

Healing, another spiritual gift highlighted in 1 Corinthians 12, serves as a testament to the Holy Spirit's ability to bring about physical and emotional restoration. Through the laying on of hands and fervent prayer, believers have witnessed the miraculous touch of the Holy Spirit, leading to the healing of ailments, the restoration of health, and the renewal of hope. The stories of these healings stand as vivid reminders of the Holy Spirit's capacity to bring forth wholeness in the midst of brokenness.

Speaking in tongues, as described in 1 Corinthians 14, is a gift that transcends linguistic boundaries, allowing believers to communicate with the divine in a language that surpasses human understanding. This gift fosters a profound connection with the Holy Spirit, creating a space for intimate communion and fervent prayer. The personal stories of individuals who have experienced the manifestation of this gift offer glimpses into the transformative power of speaking in tongues in their daily lives and spiritual journeys.

Through the exploration of these spiritual gifts and the personal testimonies of those who have embraced them, we gain insights into the vital role they play in the life of a believer and the edification of the Church. These gifts are not relics of the past but living expressions of the Holy Spirit's ongoing work, inviting believers to discover their unique gifting and actively participate in the divine plan for their lives and the world around them.

As we journey through this section, we are reminded that embracing the Holy Spirit is an invitation to unearth and embrace these gifts, allowing them to enrich our faith, empower our ministry, and deepen our relationship with the divine. It is a journey that invites us to step into the fullness of our spiritual potential, guided and empowered by the Holy Spirit.

As we continue our exploration of spiritual gifts and the transformative influence of embracing the Holy Spirit, we are invited to peer deeper into the lives of individuals whose faith journeys have been profoundly shaped by the activation and manifestation of these extraordinary gifts. These gifts, as outlined in the New Testament, are not distant relics of a bygone era but are vibrant and accessible channels through which the Holy Spirit empowers believers in their walk of faith.

The gift of prophecy, often associated with divine revelations and messages from the heavenly realm, serves as a compass guiding believers through life's intricate terrain. In the annals of Christian history and in the narratives of contemporary believers, we discover the remarkable stories of individuals who have not only received prophetic messages but have also been vessels through which these divine insights have flowed. These stories illustrate how the Holy Spirit's gift of prophecy has provided timely guidance, encouragement, and clarity in the midst of life's complexities.

Healing, another spiritual gift that holds a significant place in the arsenal of divine empowerment, is not confined to the stories of the past but is a living reality in the lives of modern believers. Through the laying on of hands, fervent prayer, and an unwavering faith in the Holy Spirit's healing touch, individuals have witnessed miraculous transformations—ailments have vanished, broken bodies have been made whole, and spirits have been renewed. These stories of healing are not mere tales but living proof of the Holy Spirit's power to bring about restoration, wholeness, and hope.

Speaking in tongues, often regarded as a deeply personal and intimate form of communication with the divine, is a gift that continues to draw believers into the depths of the Holy Spirit's presence. The experiences shared by those who have spoken in tongues reveal how this gift transcends language barriers, enabling believers to engage in fervent prayer, intercession, and communion with God on a profound level. These testimonies underscore the transformative nature of speaking in tongues, as it fosters a deeper connection with the divine and ignites a passionate pursuit of spiritual intimacy.

As we immerse ourselves in the stories of these spiritual gifts and their impact on believers' lives, we gain a deeper understanding of the vital role they play in the life of a believer and the edification of the Church.

These gifts, far from being distant and inaccessible, are manifestations of the Holy Spirit's ongoing work, inviting believers to embrace their unique spiritual calling and actively participate in the divine mission.

Through the exploration of these gifts and the personal testimonies of those who have walked this path, we are encouraged to recognize and activate these extraordinary gifts within our own lives. Embracing the Holy Spirit means embracing the gifts it bestows upon us— gifts that enrich our faith, empower our ministry, and deepen our connection with the divine. It is a journey that calls us to step into the fullness of our spiritual potential, guided and empowered by the Holy Spirit's transformative influence.

Embracing Spiritual Gifts through the Holy Spirit

In the quiet of her small prayer group, Andrea felt a tug on her heart that she couldn't ignore. She had recently heard about the spiritual gifts described in the New Testament but had assumed they were for "other people," those who seemed naturally gifted for ministry or with a special calling. But this time was different. During their meeting, someone mentioned a need for healing, and Andrea found herself overwhelmed with a compassion so strong it felt like an invitation. She didn't feel equipped—she wasn't a pastor or a healer—but she took a deep breath, placed her hand on her friend's shoulder, and quietly prayed.

As Andrea prayed, she felt a warmth flow through her, and a sense of calm settled over her. Later, her friend shared that they had experienced relief and peace beyond anything they'd felt before. Andrea couldn't believe it: God had worked through her, through her small act of faith, to bring healing to someone else.

Her journey didn't stop there. As Andrea continued to pray for guidance, she began noticing moments when the Holy Spirit nudged her with insights or words of encouragement for others. She was hesitant at first, not wanting to make mistakes or come across as presumptuous, but as she began to share these insights in love, people responded with gratitude and surprise. They found her words resonated deeply, aligning with issues they had been wrestling with in private. The Holy Spirit was using her in the gift of prophecy, guiding her to speak words of comfort and direction to those who needed them most.

And then there was her private prayer life. As she leaned more into her relationship with the Holy Spirit, Andrea experienced the gift of speaking in tongues during a moment of worship. The unfamiliar language felt strangely natural and brought a new intimacy to her prayer time, a way of connecting with God that went beyond words. It was as if her spirit was able to express things her mind could not articulate, bringing her both peace and a renewed sense of purpose.

Andrea's journey with these spiritual gifts transformed not only her relationship with God but also her role in her faith community. What she once thought were abilities reserved for the extraordinary were now ways she experienced the Holy Spirit's presence personally and deeply. She came to realize that these gifts were not about her qualifications but about her openness to the Holy Spirit's leading.

Andrea's story reminds us that the Holy Spirit equips each believer with unique gifts meant to serve others, build up the Church, and deepen our relationship with God. For anyone feeling unequipped or doubtful, her journey shows that the Holy Spirit's gifts are available to anyone willing to listen, trust, and follow. They're a reminder that within the Holy Spirit, every believer can find a source of empowerment and purpose beyond their natural limitations, lighting the way toward a life of faith enriched by these extraordinary gifts.

The Fruit of the Spirit

In the rich tapestry of the Christian faith, the fruits of the Spirit, as beautifully described in Galatians 5:22-23, emerge as a testament to the transformative power of embracing the Holy Spirit. These spiritual virtues—love, joy, peace, patience, kindness, goodness, faithfulness, gentleness, and self-control—are not mere abstract ideals but living expressions of the Holy Spirit's presence within the lives of believers. As we delve into these fruits, we encounter a profound journey of character transformation and the positive ripple effect it has on individuals and the world around them.

At the heart of this exploration lies love—the foundational fruit from which all others spring forth. Love, as illuminated in 1 Corinthians 13, is not merely an emotion but a divine force that transcends human understanding. When believers embrace the Holy Spirit, they are enveloped in a love that knows no bounds, enabling them to love not only those who are easy to love but also those who may seem unlovable. Real-life stories and practical examples abound of individuals whose lives have been utterly transformed by this radical love, breaking down barriers, healing wounds, and fostering reconciliation.

The fruit of joy is a wellspring of delight that transcends circumstances, rooted in the deep joy of salvation and a vibrant relationship with God. When believers embrace the Holy

Spirit, joy becomes a cornerstone of their lives, infusing every moment with a sense of purpose and celebration. In the face of adversity and trials, the joy that emanates from the Holy Spirit provides unwavering strength, lifting spirits and drawing others into the radiance of God's presence.

Peace, the fruit that transcends understanding, becomes a guiding light for believers who embrace the Holy Spirit. In a world marked by chaos and uncertainty, this peace anchors the soul, bringing serenity even in the midst of life's storms. Real-life stories of individuals who have walked through tumultuous times with an unshakable peace bear witness to the Holy Spirit's transformative work in cultivating this fruit.

Patience, kindness, goodness, faithfulness, gentleness, and self-control—all these fruits speak to the character transformation that occurs when believers embrace the Holy Spirit. They represent the beauty of Christlikeness, as individuals grow in their capacity to bear witness to these virtues in their daily lives. Through practical examples and personal anecdotes, we witness how these fruits impact relationships, foster harmony, and create a ripple effect of positivity and transformation in communities and beyond.

In this exploration, we celebrate the transformative power of embracing the Holy Spirit, recognizing that it is through the cultivation of these fruits that believers not only deepen their own character but also become beacons of light and love in a world hungry for hope and authenticity. The journey of embracing the Holy Spirit is a journey toward bearing spiritual fruit that enriches lives, transforms hearts, and leaves an indelible mark on the world.

As we continue to traverse the landscape of the fruits of the Spirit and their transformative impact when embracing the Holy Spirit, we are guided into a deeper understanding of these virtues and their profound relevance in our lives.

Kindness, an exquisite facet of the fruit of the Spirit, manifests itself in actions that extend compassion and grace to others. When believers wholeheartedly embrace the Holy Spirit, they find themselves becoming conduits of kindness, radiating warmth and goodwill. Through real-life stories and practical examples, we encounter individuals whose simple acts of kindness have had a ripple effect, creating a culture of empathy and generosity.

Goodness, closely intertwined with kindness, speaks to a moral uprightness that is birthed from the indwelling of the Holy Spirit. Those who embrace the Spirit find themselves drawn toward goodness, discerning right from wrong and choosing the path of integrity. The stories of individuals who have undergone moral transformation illuminate the profound impact of goodness in navigating ethical dilemmas and making a positive mark in the world.

Faithfulness, an enduring quality rooted in trustworthiness and commitment, shines brightly in the lives of those who embrace the Holy Spirit. As we delve into personal narratives, we encounter individuals who have remained steadfast in their faith and unwavering in their devotion, even in the face of adversity. The fruit of faithfulness becomes a beacon of hope and consistency in a world marked by shifting sands.

Gentleness, a gentle and humble spirit that bears witness to the meekness of Christ, emerges as a hallmark of believers who embrace the Holy Spirit. Real-life stories highlight how gentleness can mend relationships, soothe conflicts, and foster an atmosphere of harmony. It is through the fruit of gentleness that the transformative power of the Holy Spirit is most profoundly experienced in personal interactions.

Self-control, the final jewel in the crown of the fruits of the Spirit, serves as a bulwark against impulsive and destructive behaviors. When individuals wholeheartedly embrace the Holy Spirit, they find themselves endowed with the capacity for self-control, enabling them to overcome temptations and destructive habits. These stories of triumph over self-destructive patterns serve as a testament to the Holy Spirit's ability to empower believers to live a life of discipline and purpose.

In the examination of these fruits, we gain a deeper appreciation for the transformative influence of embracing the Holy Spirit. These virtues are not mere ideals but living expressions of the Holy Spirit's ongoing work in the lives of believers. They serve as a testament to the profound character transformation that takes place when the Holy Spirit is welcomed into one's heart and life.

As we journey through this exploration, we are invited to embrace the Holy Spirit with open hearts and minds, allowing these fruits to take root and flourish in our lives. It is through the cultivation of these virtues that believers not only deepen their relationship with the divine but also become agents of positive change, bringing light and transformation to a world in need of love, joy, peace, patience, kindness, goodness, faithfulness, gentleness, and self-control.

―――――――――

A Life Transformed by the Fruits of the Spirit

For years, Ben had built walls around his heart. A childhood marked by hardship and mistrust had taught him to rely only on himself, and he was quick-tempered, skeptical of others, and often burdened by worry. But everything changed when he encountered a community of believers who welcomed him with open arms. These people radiated a warmth he couldn't quite understand—a love that seemed to shine from somewhere deep within them. Intrigued, he kept coming back, drawn by their patience, kindness, and unexplainable peace.

As Ben started to open up, he felt a tug on his heart. The messages he heard about the Holy Spirit's transforming power spoke directly to his wounded soul, and one day, he surrendered his life to Christ. That was when his true transformation began.

Over time, Ben felt a shift in his outlook and reactions. Where he once responded with anger, he now found himself responding with gentleness. Patience, a virtue he never thought he'd embody, began to take root in his life. When a coworker wronged him, he felt a calm he didn't recognize and chose forgiveness. "This isn't me," he thought, marveling at how the Holy Spirit was softening his once-hardened heart.

One evening, Ben's young niece visited, teary-eyed after being bullied at school. In the past, he might have dismissed her emotions or told her to toughen up. But this time, he knelt beside her, offering words of kindness and comfort. His gentleness soothed her, and she hugged him, saying, "I feel better, Uncle Ben. Thank you." The Holy Spirit's work in his life was radiating to those around him, fostering connections he'd never thought possible.

Ben's family noticed the change. His mother, who had seen his temper and mistrust as a young man, was amazed at his newfound self-control and joy. Conversations once marked by tension and misunderstandings became warm and heartfelt. Ben was even able to share with his family the transformation he'd experienced, pointing to the Holy Spirit as the source of his peace and strength.

Today, Ben's life reflects the fruits of the Spirit. His relationships are no longer strained but grounded in kindness, gentleness, and faithfulness. His heart is free from the worry that once plagued him, replaced by a joy rooted not in circumstances but in a deep connection with God. And as he continues to grow, the Spirit's fruits spread from his life to those around him, creating a ripple effect of hope and transformation.

Ben's story is a testament to the Holy Spirit's power to cultivate the fruits of love, joy, peace, patience, kindness, goodness, faithfulness, gentleness, and self-control. His journey shows us that the fruits of the Spirit are not just virtues to aspire to but living expressions of God's work in us. When we embrace the Holy Spirit, we are invited into a life that transforms us and touches others, making us agents of light and love in a world hungry for hope.

———

Conclusion

As we draw the final curtain on Chapter 8, we find ourselves bathed in the radiant glow of transformation—a transformation made possible by the embrace of the Holy Spirit. This chapter, titled "A Life Transformed: The Tenfold Impact of Embracing the Holy Spirit," has been a journey through the remarkable landscapes of faith, character, and spiritual gifts. It has been a testament to the boundless power of the divine force that resides within us when we welcome the Holy Spirit into our lives.

In our exploration of this spiritual odyssey, we have witnessed the incredible resilience that emerges when believers embrace the Holy Spirit. Challenges that once loomed as insurmountable obstacles have been conquered, and the human spirit has soared to new heights. Through the real-life stories and practical examples that have graced these pages, we have seen that the Holy Spirit not only empowers but also renews, reinvigorates, and revitalizes every facet of our existence.

Furthermore, we have uncovered the exquisite tapestry of spiritual fruit that blossoms when we embrace the Holy Spirit. Love, joy, peace, patience, kindness, goodness, faithfulness, gentleness, and self-control—these are not mere ideals but living expressions of the Spirit's work within us. These virtues have the power to transform not only our character but also the very essence of our relationships, communities, and the world.

And let us not forget the awe-inspiring realm of spiritual gifts that unfolds when we fully embrace the Holy Spirit. Through prophecy, healing, speaking in tongues, and other extraordinary manifestations, we have glimpsed the limitless potential that awaits those who welcome the Spirit into their lives. These gifts are not relics of the past but a dynamic force that enriches our personal faith journeys and empowers us to be instruments of divine light in a world in need.

As we conclude this chapter, we are reminded that embracing the Holy Spirit is not a destination but a continuous journey-an ongoing partnership with the divine. It is an invitation to a life that transcends the ordinary, a life marked by spiritual growth, unwavering character, and the radiant glow of spiritual gifts. It is a journey that redefines our understanding of faith, love, and limitless potential.

As we conclude this chapter, we are reminded that embracing the Holy Spirit is not a destination but a continuous journey—an ongoing partnership with the divine. It is an invitation to a life that transcends the ordinary, a life marked by spiritual growth, unwavering character, and the radiant glow of spiritual gifts. It is a journey that redefines our understanding of faith, love, and limitless potential.

So, dear reader, may this chapter be a source of inspiration and encouragement as you continue to embrace the Holy Spirit in your own life. May it serve as a reminder that the impact of the Spirit knows no bounds, and that when we partner with the divine, our lives are forever transformed, and we become beacons of hope and light in a world hungering for authenticity and divine presence. As we bid farewell to Chapter 8, may the transformative journey of embracing the Holy Spirit continue to unfold, bringing new depths of faith, joy, and purpose with each step we take.

CHAPTER NINE

Prayerful Whispers: The Intimacy of Praying in Tongues and Its Benefits

"In the same way, the Spirit helps us in our weakness. We do not know what we ought to pray for, but the Spirit Himself intercedes for us through wordless groans." — ROMANS 8:26 NIV

I n the sacred realm of prayer, there exists a language that transcends human understanding— a language of the spirit, a language of intimacy, a language known as "praying in tongues." As we embark on Chapter 9, titled "Prayerful Whispers: The Intimacy of Praying in Tongues and Its Benefits," we step into a realm where the divine and the human meet in an extraordinary exchange of whispers.

In the hush of quiet moments and the fervor of intercession, believers across generations have discovered the profound mystery and spiritual significance of this sacred practice. It is a language that bypasses the limitations of words, allowing the soul to commune directly with the Divine. Within its syllables and sounds, we find a connection that defies language barriers, a communion that touches the deepest recesses of the soul.

This chapter invites us to explore the intricacies of praying in tongues; to uncover the transformative power it holds for personal growth and intimacy with God, and to witness its role as a formidable weapon in intercession and spiritual warfare. Through personal testimonies, biblical insights, and a journey into the hearts of believers, we will uncover the hidden treasures of this sacred language, understanding its benefits, and discovering how it opens doors to profound intimacy with the Divine. It is an invitation to a deeper, more intimate walk with God through the prayerful whispers of the heart.

The Mystery of Praying in Tongues

In the enchanting realm of spiritual practices, few are as mysterious and spiritually enriching as the gift of praying in tongues. In this opening topic of Chapter 9, we embark on a profound exploration of "The Mystery of Praying in Tongues." Our journey begins with the firm foundation of Scripture, as we draw insights from passages such as 1 Corinthians 14 and

Romans 8:26-27. These sacred texts unveil the heart of this divine language—a language that transcends mere human words and speaks directly to the depths of the soul.

As we delve deeper into the heart of this enigmatic practice, we uncover the beautiful truth that praying in tongues offers believers a unique and intimate connection with the Divine. It's a form of prayer that bypasses the limitations of human language, allowing the soul to commune directly with God's heart. In these moments, we find ourselves immersed in a sacred dialogue, where the Spirit intercedes on our behalf with groanings too deep for words, as Romans 8:26-27 beautifully illustrates.

This mysterious gift of praying in tongues has the power to transport us beyond the boundaries of the natural world and into the supernatural embrace of the divine. It is an intimate conversation that transcends language barriers, and as we venture further into its depths, we discover that it is indeed a profound way to connect with the very heart of God Himself.

As we immerse ourselves further into "The Mystery of Praying in Tongues," we come to recognize that this sacred practice is not bound by the limitations of human understanding. Instead, it invites believers into a realm where words alone cannot express the depths of their hearts' desires, joys, and sorrows. Praying in tongues becomes the language of the soul, allowing for a direct and unfiltered connection with the divine.

1 Corinthians 14 guides us along this journey, emphasizing the edifying nature of praying in tongues and its ability to build up the individual believer's spirit. It is in these moments of intimate communion with God that we experience the profound transformation of our innermost being. The mystery of praying in tongues becomes a powerful expression of faith—a faith that transcends the natural realm and ventures into the supernatural.

As we navigate this mystical terrain, we find ourselves drawn closer to the heart of God. The beauty of this practice lies not only in its mystery but also in its ability to foster a deeper, more intimate relationship with the divine. In the quiet whispers of tongues, we discover a profound language of love— a language that brings us into the very presence of God and envelops us in His boundless grace. So, dear reader, as we continue to explore this captivating mystery, may your heart be open to the profound and transformative experience of praying in tongues, where words may fail, but the spirit soars in the embrace of the divine.

In our ongoing exploration of "The Mystery of Praying in Tongues," we find ourselves on a sacred journey, a journey that transcends the limitations of human language and reaches deep into the soul's longing for communion with the divine. This practice, rooted in the rich soil of biblical truth, goes beyond the superficial and takes us into the depths of spiritual intimacy.

The beauty of praying in tongues lies in its ability to convey the inexpressible. When our hearts overflow with gratitude, when our souls ache with longing, or when we face trials beyond words, tongues become the vessel through which our deepest emotions and desires are laid bare before God. The apostle Paul's words in 1 Corinthians 14 underscore the edification that takes place in this intimate exchange between the believer and the Creator. It is a sacred language that fosters personal growth, spiritual renewal, and an unbreakable connection with the divine.

As we journey through the mysterious landscape of praying in tongues, let us remain open to the profound and life-changing experiences that await us. In the quiet moments of this practice, we discover a depth of relationship with God that is beyond words—an intimacy that transcends the ordinary and elevates our spirits to new heights. It is a mystery worth exploring, a gift worth cherishing, and a journey worth embarking upon, for in the profound mystery of praying in tongues, we find ourselves drawn closer to the heart of God, where words may fade, but the spirit soars.

———

A Journey Into the Heart of God Through
Praying in Tongues

Bailey had always considered herself a person of deep faith, attending church regularly and reading Scripture daily. But as her life became filled with stress and overwhelming challenges, she found herself at a loss for words when she tried to pray. Her prayers seemed repetitive, and she felt disconnected, yearning for something more—a deeper communion with God that went beyond the limits of language.

One evening, after a particularly difficult day, Bailey sat alone in her room, feeling the weight of unspoken emotions pressing down on her heart. She opened her Bible to Romans 8:26-27, where she read, "The Spirit helps us in our weakness. We do not know what we ought to pray for, but the Spirit himself intercedes for us with groanings too deep for words." She felt a longing rise within her, an urge to surrender her inability to articulate her feelings and allow the Holy Spirit to lead her in a new way of praying.

As she began to pray, something unexpected happened. A gentle, unfamiliar language began to flow from her lips—a language that felt like it bypassed her mind and reached straight into her spirit. Bailey was startled at first, but then a profound peace washed over her. She continued, letting the words flow freely, feeling the Holy Spirit's presence envelop her with a warmth she had never experienced. It was as if she were speaking directly to God in a language only her heart and His could understand.

Over time, praying in tongues became a regular part of Bailey's spiritual life. Whenever she felt overwhelmed, lost, or even just grateful beyond words, she would retreat to a quiet place and allow her spirit to commune with God in this sacred, mysterious language. She found that praying in tongues brought her peace, clarity, and a sense of release that was unlike any prayer she had ever known.

The change in Bailey's life was noticeable to those around her. Friends and family saw a newfound resilience in her—a calmness that remained unshaken, even during tough situations. Where she had once struggled with stress and anxiety, she now seemed anchored, grounded by a strength that others sensed but couldn't quite place.

Bailey's journey with praying in tongues became a source of personal transformation, bringing healing to areas of her life she hadn't known needed it. She found herself growing in compassion and empathy, reaching out to those around her with a depth of kindness that came from the wellspring of her own renewed heart.

Praying in tongues, once a mystery, had become a doorway to an intimate relationship with God. In those moments of unspoken communion, she felt her spirit intertwined with His, speaking without words, sharing without reservation. It was as if she had found a direct line to the heart of God—a line that bypassed all language and entered straight into His presence.

Bailey's story reminds us that praying in tongues is more than a mystical experience; it's a gift of intimate communion, a way to express the inexpressible and pour out our hearts directly to God. Through this profound practice, Bailey discovered a new depth of peace and resilience, a reminder that the Holy Spirit's presence is always there, guiding us, comforting us, and drawing us closer to the heart of God where words may fail, but the spirit soars.

―――――――

Benefits for Personal Spiritual Growth

In the realm of spiritual growth and intimacy with the Divine, few practices hold the transformative power that praying in tongues does. As we delve into the second topic of Chapter 9, "Benefits for Personal Spiritual Growth," we embark on a journey that illuminates the profound impact of this sacred practice on the lives of believers.

Praying in tongues becomes a conduit for spiritual breakthroughs that transcend the ordinary. It is in these moments of communion with the Divine that believers often experience a heightened sensitivity to the guidance of the Holy Spirit. As 1 Corinthians 14:2 reminds us, "For one who speaks in a tongue speaks not to men but to God; for no one understands him, but he utters mysteries in the Spirit." This unique form of prayer allows us to access the deep recesses of our souls, where the Spirit intercedes on our behalf, articulating our unspoken desires and needs before the Creator.

Through the personal testimonies and stories shared within these pages, you'll encounter believers who have walked the path of spiritual growth through praying in tongues. These individuals have witnessed firsthand the transformative power of this practice as they journeyed toward a deeper intimacy with God. They testify to a heightened awareness of God's love, a profound sense of His presence, and a stronger connection to His heart.

As you delve deeper into this topic, you'll discover that praying in tongues is not just a language of the soul; it is a spiritual discipline that fosters growth, nurtures intimacy, and kindles a more profound relationship with the Divine. It is an invitation to experience the depths of God's love and a means to journey deeper into His embrace.

In the quiet moments of praying in tongues, believers often find themselves on a spiritual journey like no other. It is a journey that transcends the ordinary and reaches into the extraordinary-the realm of heightened spiritual sensitivity and divine connection. As believers open themselves to the gift of praying in tongues, they step into a sacred space where the mysteries of the Spirit are unveiled, and the soul's deepest yearnings are expressed.

One of the remarkable aspects of this practice is its ability to create spiritual breakthroughs in the lives of those who engage in it. The apostle Paul, in 1 Corinthians 14, speaks of the profound mysteries that unfold when one prays in tongues. It is as if a door to the spiritual realm swings open, allowing believers to pour out their hearts in a language only understood by God. Through this language of the soul, they articulate their deepest desires, fears, and hopes, creating a bridge between the finite and the infinite.

Within these pages, you will encounter the powerful stories of believers who have experienced these spiritual breakthroughs firsthand. Their testimonies are a testament to the transformative power of praying in tongues. They speak of moments when the burdens of life were lifted, when clarity emerged from confusion, and when a tangible sense of God's presence enveloped them. These experiences serve as a reminder that through this sacred practice, believers can grow spiritually, drawing closer to the heart of God and gaining a deeper understanding of His love.

Indeed, the benefits of praying in tongues for personal spiritual growth are vast and profound. It is a practice that invites believers into a more profound relationship with the Divine—a relationship where the language of the soul finds its voice, where the Spirit intercedes on their behalf, and where the mysteries of God's love are unveiled in ever-deepening layers.

So, dear reader, as you journey through the stories and insights shared within this chapter, may you find inspiration and encouragement to embrace the transformative power of praying in tongues for your own spiritual growth and intimacy with God.

The Transformative Power of Praying in Tongues

For many years, Autumn felt that her faith had reached a plateau. She read her Bible, attended church, and prayed daily, but a sense of stagnation lingered. Her prayers began to feel repetitive, and she found herself yearning for a deeper connection with God, a way to express the unspoken longings of her heart that words just couldn't seem to capture.

One evening at a prayer gathering, Autumn's pastor shared about the power and purpose of praying in tongues, citing 1 Corinthians 14:2: "For one who speaks in a tongue speaks not to men but to God; for no one understands him, but he utters mysteries in the Spirit." As the pastor described how praying in tongues allows the Holy Spirit to communicate through us when words fall short, Autumn felt a gentle nudge in her heart, a call to open herself to this spiritual gift.

At first, she was hesitant, unsure of what to expect. But later that night, alone in her quiet room, Autumn knelt and asked God to guide her. As she began to pray, she felt an unfamiliar language rise within her—a language that bypassed her mind and flowed directly from her spirit. As the words spilled out, a profound sense of peace and release filled her, as if she had finally found a way to pour out the deepest parts of herself to God. It was a sacred language beyond words, a connection she had never experienced before.

In the days that followed, Autumn continued to incorporate praying in tongues into her daily devotions. She noticed an undeniable shift within herself: moments of fear and doubt were met with newfound peace, her prayers felt alive and heartfelt, and she sensed God's guidance more clearly than ever. She found that in times of stress or confusion, this intimate form of prayer brought her a calm assurance, reminding her that the Holy Spirit was interceding for her, articulating her needs in ways she couldn't.

Autumn's spiritual journey took on a vibrant new dimension. Her faith grew deeper, her trust in God expanded, and she felt empowered in her everyday life, even in difficult situations. She became more aware of God's love, not just as a concept but as a daily presence guiding her heart and mind. Friends and family noticed her transformation—a newfound patience, joy, and confidence that radiated in her interactions.

Through her journey of praying in tongues, Autumn experienced firsthand the benefits of this sacred gift. It deepened her relationship with God, heightened her sensitivity to the Holy Spirit, and allowed her to express the inexpressible, to release burdens she hadn't realized she was carrying. Praying in tongues had opened the door to a spiritual growth she once thought was beyond her reach.

Autumn's story is a testament to the power of praying in tongues as a tool for personal spiritual growth. It's a reminder that when words fail, the Holy Spirit provides a language of the soul that reaches the heart of God. For Autumn, it became a pathway to a vibrant, deeper relationship with her Creator—a journey that continues to inspire her, knowing that the mysteries of God's love and guidance are always within reach.

The Role of Praying in Tongues in Intercession and Spiritual Warfare

In the realm of spiritual warfare and intercessory prayer, believers wield a formidable weapon—the gift of praying in tongues. As we delve into the third topic of Chapter 9, "The Role of Praying in Tongues in Intercession and Spiritual Warfare," we embark on a journey that reveals the profound significance of this practice in confronting spiritual battles and dismantling strongholds.

At the heart of this discussion lies the biblical concept of "praying in the Spirit," a concept that carries tremendous weight in the realm of spiritual warfare. Ephesians 6:18 exhorts believers to "pray at all times in the Spirit, with all prayer and supplication." This divine directive points to the unique and powerful role that praying in tongues plays in intercessory prayer and spiritual warfare. It is a language that transcends human understanding and taps into the very heart and mind of God.

Throughout these pages, you will encounter stories of individuals who have harnessed the power of praying in tongues in the battle against spiritual adversaries and insurmountable challenges. These testimonies serve as living proof of the miraculous answers to prayer and the breakthroughs that can be attained through this practice. Believers have witnessed strongholds crumble, chains of bondage shatter, and the impossible become possible when they engaged in intercession and spiritual warfare through the language of tongues.

As we explore this topic, we come to understand that praying in tongues is not merely a spiritual exercise; it is a potent weapon that equips believers to stand firm in the face of adversity and to engage in warfare against the forces of darkness. It is a language that allows the Spirit to intercede on our behalf with groanings too deep for words, as Romans 8:26-27 beautifully illustrates. In these moments of spiritual battle, praying in tongues becomes a beacon of hope, a source of divine guidance, and a channel through which the miraculous unfolds.

May the stories and insights shared within this chapter serve as a source of inspiration and empowerment, reminding us of the profound role that praying in tongues plays in intercession and spiritual warfare. It is a practice that invites believers to rise up, take their place on the battlefield, and witness the triumph of light over darkness, all through the intimate and powerful language of the Spirit.

As we journey through the stories of believers who have harnessed the power of praying in tongues for intercession and spiritual warfare, we encounter firsthand accounts of divine intervention and triumphant victories. These testimonies serve as a testament to the reality that when believers engage in this sacred practice, they become partners with the Holy Spirit in confronting and overcoming the forces of darkness.

In the realm of spiritual warfare, the language of tongues becomes a mighty weapon, piercing through the darkness with the light of God's truth and power. It is a language that aligns with the heart of God, offering prayers that are perfectly attuned to His divine will. Romans 8:26-27 assures us of this: "Likewise, the Spirit helps us in our weakness. For we do not know what to pray for as we ought, but the Spirit himself intercedes for us with groanings too deep for words."

Through these groanings of the Spirit, believers have witnessed miracles unfold. They have seen the chains of addiction shattered, the bonds of oppression broken, and the captives set free. They have stood in the gap for loved ones, cities, and nations, and witnessed transformation on a grand scale. They have discovered that in the practice of praying in tongues, there is a divine partnership—an alignment with God's purposes that brings about extraordinary results.

As we conclude our exploration of this topic, may you be inspired by the stories of believers who have harnessed the power of praying in tongues for intercession and spiritual warfare. May you be reminded that this sacred language is not merely a spiritual exercise but a divine weapon, an intimate connection with the heart of God, and a means through which the impossible becomes possible. In the battle against darkness, it is a beacon of hope, a wellspring of strength, and a testament to the victory that believers can claim through the language of the Spirit.

The Power of Praying in Tongues in Spiritual Warfare

Ahab had faced what seemed like an insurmountable wall in his life. For years, he struggled with an oppressive darkness—a sense of hopelessness and despair that seemed to settle over him like a storm cloud. No matter how hard he tried, he couldn't shake it, and as a believer, he felt a sense of frustration and guilt for not being able to find peace. He knew he was in a spiritual battle, but the usual prayers he recited seemed to fall short of breaking through the darkness.

One evening, in a moment of desperation, Ahab felt a nudge in his spirit to pray differently. Recalling his pastor's words on the power of praying in tongues in times of intense spiritual warfare, he knelt down and asked the Holy Spirit to lead him in prayer. Slowly, an unfamiliar language began to rise within him—a language he didn't understand but felt deep in his spirit. As he continued to pray, he felt a surge of strength and resilience he hadn't experienced before. It was as if he'd entered a new realm of prayer, one that transcended his own understanding and allowed him to express the deepest parts of his heart.

As the days went on, Ahab continued to pray in tongues regularly. He would pray this way whenever he felt the weight of darkness looming over him. He began to sense the power of the Holy Spirit working on his behalf, pushing back the forces that had bound him for so long. Over time, he noticed tangible changes in his life: moments of peace replaced his anxiety, his thoughts became clearer, and a sense of freedom began to take root in his heart. It was as if the oppressive stronghold over his life was being dismantled piece by piece.

But the story didn't end there. Ahab's spiritual breakthrough began to impact his family and friends as well. One night, his younger sister called him, struggling with issues he recognized—anxiety, hopelessness, and fear. Without hesitation, Ahab prayed with her, this time in tongues, allowing the Holy Spirit to intercede through him. His sister, too, began to experience peace and strength that she hadn't felt before, and soon she began to seek a closer relationship with God.

Ahab's journey through praying in tongues for intercession and spiritual warfare transformed not only his life but also those around him. He found that this sacred practice was more than just a personal exercise; it was a powerful tool that aligned his spirit with the will of God, allowing him to partner with the Holy Spirit to bring light into dark places.

Ahab's story stands as a testament to the potent role that praying in tongues plays in spiritual warfare. It highlights how this divine language goes beyond words, empowering believers to confront and overcome the darkness through a direct connection with God's heart. For Ahab, praying in tongues became the key to breaking through spiritual strongholds, opening the way for transformation, and establishing a legacy of faith and resilience. His journey reminds us that when we engage with the Holy Spirit through the language of tongues, we are not fighting alone but standing alongside a mighty force that brings light, healing, and victory.

Conclusion

In the quietude of prayerful whispers, we have traversed the sacred landscape of praying in tongues and its profound benefits. As we conclude Chapter 9, we emerge from this journey with a deeper understanding of the intimacy and power encapsulated within this divine language.

Throughout the pages of this chapter, we have encountered the mysterious beauty of a language that transcends the limitations of words. We have seen how it opens doors to a profound connection with the Divine—a connection that touches the depths of the soul. It is a language that defies language barriers, allowing believers to engage in a direct and intimate communion with their Creator.

We have explored the transformative power of praying in tongues, witnessing the spiritual growth and personal renewal it brings to those who embrace it. It is a practice that deepens our relationship with God, unveiling His love and wisdom in ever-deeper layers. Through the personal stories shared within these pages, we have seen how believers have experienced spiritual breakthroughs, heightened sensitivity to the Holy Spirit's guidance, and an abiding sense of God's presence.

Additionally, we have delved into the role of praying in tongues as a formidable weapon in intercession and spiritual warfare. This language of the Spirit becomes a beacon of hope in the midst of spiritual battles, a channel through which divine intervention occurs, and a means to confront strongholds with supernatural power. We have heard stories of miraculous answers to prayer and triumphant victories achieved through this sacred practice.

As we bid farewell to Chapter 9, may we carry with us the understanding that praying in tongues is not a mere exercise but a profound privilege— a divine invitation to an intimate encounter with God. It is a language that speaks to the depths of our being and resonates with the heart of the Almighty. In the sacred whispers of this language, we find solace, strength, and an unbreakable bond with the Divine. May it continue to be a source of intimacy, transformation, and empowerment in our spiritual journeys, as we embrace the profound mysteries of praying in tongues.

Living the Spirit Filled Life: Daily Walking in the Power and Guidance of the Holy Spirit

"Since we live by the Spirit, let us keep in step with the Spirit."
— GALATIANS 5:25 NIV

In the previous chapters of our journey through the Spirit-filled life, we've explored the promises, the power, and the transformative work of the Holy Spirit. We've witnessed how embracing the Spirit can lead to a deeper understanding of God's love, an activation of spiritual gifts, and a life marked by the fruits of the Spirit. But now, we come to the culmination of our exploration—the practical application of living a Spirit-filled life every day.

In this final chapter, we embark on a journey into the ordinary moments of life, where the extraordinary presence of the Holy Spirit continues to guide, empower, and transform. This is where the rubber meets the road, where theology becomes a lived experience, and where the unseen force of divine power manifests in the midst of our daily routines.

Join me as we delve into the role of the Holy Spirit in our everyday existence. We'll explore how the Spirit empowers us to navigate the complexities of life, cultivate a Spirit-filled lifestyle, and walk in obedience to His gentle guidance. Through stories, insights, and practical wisdom, we'll discover the profound beauty of living each day in the power and presence of the Holy Spirit, where even the most mundane moments become sacred encounters with the divine. Welcome to the journey of daily walking in the Spirit's embrace.

The Role of the Holy Spirit in Daily Life

In the ebb and flow of our daily lives, the presence of the Holy Spirit is not a distant or abstract concept but a tangible reality. It is in the midst of our ordinary moments that the Holy Spirit stands as our constant guide and companion. Scripture reminds us in Proverbs 3:5-6, "Trust in the Lord with all your heart and lean not on your own understanding; in all your ways submit to him, and he will make your paths straight." This truth underscores the profound role of the Holy Spirit in our daily existence.

Consider the times when you've faced challenging decisions, unsure of which path to take. It is the Holy Spirit who whispers wisdom into our hearts, offering clarity and direction. When we encounter the storms of life, it is the Spirit who provides the calm assurance and comfort that surpasses human understanding. And in the mundane routines of each day, the Spirit's presence is an ever-present source of inspiration and guidance. Whether it's a simple choice, a complex decision, or a moment of uncertainty, the Holy Spirit is our steady compass, pointing us toward the path of righteousness and truth.

The Holy Spirit does not confine His guidance to grandiose moments of revelation but extends His divine assistance to the minutiae of our lives. It is in the daily walk, the routine of existence, and the ordinary decisions that the Spirit's influence is most profoundly felt. So, let us embark on this exploration of the Holy Spirit's role in our daily lives, unveiling the practical insights, real-life examples, and personal experiences that illuminate the path He sets before us. As we journey together, may we discover the transformative power of embracing the Holy Spirit in the everyday.

In the tapestry of our daily existence, the Holy Spirit weaves threads of divine guidance, revealing Himself as the silent yet ever-present force shaping our journey. Just as a shepherd leads his flock through treacherous terrain, so does the Spirit guide us through the complexities of modern life. Romans 8:26 reminds us that "the Spirit helps us in our weakness. We do not know what we ought to pray for, but the Spirit himself intercedes for us through wordless groans." This divine intercession goes beyond words; it transcends our understanding and touches the deepest recesses of our hearts.

Consider the moments when you've stood at the crossroads of life, uncertain of the right direction. It is the Holy Spirit who whispers in those quiet moments, urging us to trust in God's wisdom and lean not on our own understanding. In times of adversity, the Spirit provides solace and courage, reminding us that we are not alone in our struggles. And in the joyful moments, the Spirit rejoices with us, for He is intimately acquainted with the intricacies of our emotions and desires.

As we explore the practical implications of the Holy Spirit's role in our daily lives, we will encounter real-life stories that illuminate the path of divine guidance. From the simplest choices to the most complex decisions, the Holy Spirit's presence is an unwavering source of wisdom and comfort. So, let us embark on this journey together, unearthing the treasure trove of insights and experiences that demonstrate the Holy Spirit's profound influence on our daily walk. In the mundane and the extraordinary, may His guidance continue to light our way.

$$=========$$

Embracing the Holy Spirit in Everyday Decisions

Angela was a busy mother of three, balancing work, family, and the everyday challenges that came with both. Most of her days felt like a whirlwind, a constant stream of tasks, decisions, and responsibilities. One particularly hectic morning, she found herself overwhelmed with uncertainty. Between work issues, her children's needs, and a difficult decision regarding a friend in need, Angela felt pulled in so many directions that she didn't know where to begin.

As she sank into her kitchen chair, Angela remembered the advice of a close friend: "Invite the Holy Spirit into everything, even the small decisions." She had always associated the Holy Spirit with big, life-changing moments but hadn't considered how He might guide her in the day-to-day challenges she faced.

So, Angela closed her eyes, took a deep breath, and simply prayed, "Holy Spirit, I need Your wisdom. Guide me today." She felt a sudden sense of calm wash over her as she surrendered her plans and opened herself to divine direction.

Throughout that day, Angela noticed subtle shifts. When her youngest child began crying just as she was preparing to leave for an important meeting, she felt a nudge to take an extra moment with him instead of rushing out the door. That small choice brought comfort to her son, and she made it to her meeting with time to spare. Later, at work, an unexpected solution came to her mind that resolved a project issue that had been bothering her for weeks. As she left the office, she felt that same gentle prompting to reach out to her friend and offer her presence, realizing that this was what her friend truly needed.

Through these small, seemingly ordinary choices, Angela experienced the Holy Spirit guiding her in a way that brought peace, clarity, and a sense of purpose to her day. By allowing herself to listen for the Spirit's whisper, she found that her steps were directed, and her heart was aligned with God's wisdom.

Angela's story serves as a reminder that the Holy Spirit is not only present in our monumental life choices but also in the small, everyday moments that shape our journey. It's in these decisions—both big and small—that we see the Spirit as a gentle guide, providing clarity and comfort in the midst of life's complexities. Angela's day, though ordinary in its rhythm, became extraordinary through her choice to invite the Holy Spirit into her routine. Her experience reminds us that the Spirit's guidance is always available, a steady companion leading us through life's intricate tapestry, one thread at a time.

Cultivating a Spirit-Filled Lifestyle

Cultivating a Spirit-filled lifestyle is not a mere aspiration; it's a deliberate choice that transforms the ordinary into the extraordinary. It's about embracing the Holy Spirit as an ever-present companion on this incredible journey of faith. In

Galatians 5:25, we are encouraged to "keep in step with the Spirit," an invitation to walk in rhythm with the divine. It's not a sporadic encounter but a daily practice, an intentional decision to invite the Spirit's guidance into every facet of our existence.

Imagine your day as a canvas waiting to be painted with the vibrant colors of the Spirit. Every decision, interaction, and thought becomes an opportunity to engage with the divine. It begins with prayer, that sacred dialogue where we pour out our hearts, seeking the Spirit's wisdom and guidance. Prayer isn't confined to grandiose petitions but extends to the simplest of conversations, like a whisper to a trusted friend.

Meditation on Scripture becomes our compass, grounding us in the timeless wisdom of God's Word. In the quiet moments of reflection, the Spirit breathes life into those ancient words, revealing fresh insights and relevance for today's challenges. As we dwell on Scripture, we are, as Psalm 1:2-3 suggests, "like a tree planted by streams of water, which yields its fruit in season and whose leaf does not wither." Our minds become fertile soil, bearing the fruit of the Spirit's guidance.

Maintaining a daily connection with the Holy Spirit requires intentionality. It's about setting aside time to listen, to be still, and to heed the gentle nudges of the divine. It's acknowledging that our human understanding is limited, but the Spirit's wisdom is boundless. As we learn to surrender our will to His leading, we embark on a transformative journey, where character is refined, relationships are enriched, and decision-making is infused with divine wisdom.

So, let us explore the practical steps and mindset shifts that pave the way for a Spirit-filled lifestyle. From morning prayers to daily meditation, from conscious listening to obedient response, may we find ourselves walking in step with the Spirit, living each day in the light of His guidance.

Cultivating a Spirit-filled lifestyle is not a mere aspiration; it's a deliberate choice that transforms the ordinary into the extraordinary. It's about embracing the Holy Spirit as an ever-present companion on this incredible journey of faith. In Galatians 5:25, we are encouraged to "keep in step with the Spirit," an invitation to walk in rhythm with the divine. It's not a sporadic encounter but a daily practice, an intentional decision to invite the Spirit's guidance into every facet of our existence.

Imagine your day as a canvas waiting to be painted with the vibrant colors of the Spirit. Every decision, interaction, and thought becomes an opportunity to engage with the divine. It begins with prayer, that sacred dialogue where we pour out our hearts, seeking the Spirit's wisdom and guidance. Prayer isn't confined to grandiose petitions but extends to the simplest of conversations, like a whisper to a trusted friend.

Meditation on Scripture becomes our compass, grounding us in the timeless wisdom of God's Word. In the quiet moments of reflection, the Spirit breathes life into those ancient words, revealing fresh insights and relevance for today's challenges. As we dwell on Scripture, we are, as Psalm 1:2-3 suggests, "like a tree planted by streams of water, which yields its fruit in season and whose leaf does not wither." Our minds become fertile soil, bearing the fruit of the Spirit's guidance.

Maintaining a daily connection with the Holy Spirit requires intentionality. It's about setting aside time to listen, to be still, and to heed the gentle nudges of the divine. It's acknowledging that our human understanding is limited, but the Spirit's wisdom is boundless. As we learn to surrender our will to His leading, we embark on a transformative journey, where character is refined, relationships are enriched, and decision-making is infused with divine wisdom.

So, let us explore the practical steps and mindset shifts that pave the way for a Spirit-filled lifestyle. From morning prayers to daily meditation, from conscious listening to obedient response, may we find ourselves walking in step with the Spirit, living each day in the light of His guidance.

―――――

Choosing to Walk in Step with the Spirit

When Annabelle decided to deepen her walk of faith, she knew it meant more than attending Sunday services and reading devotionals. She wanted to live her entire life in harmony with the Holy Spirit—to cultivate a Spirit-filled lifestyle. Inspired by

Galatians 5:25, which encourages believers to "keep in step with the Spirit," she committed to this journey, aware that it would require both intention and surrender.

Annabelle started each morning in prayer, a quiet conversation with the Holy Spirit where she invited Him to guide her decisions and thoughts. This wasn't a formal or grandiose ritual but rather a simple, heartfelt dialogue. She asked for wisdom in her relationships, patience in her work, and peace in her heart. Over time, she noticed that her mornings had a new sense of calm and direction, as if she were moving to the gentle rhythm of divine guidance.

In the evening, Annabelle took time to meditate on Scripture, allowing the Holy Spirit to breathe life into familiar verses. She'd often read a passage she'd known for years and find new insights, moments of revelation that spoke directly to her challenges and needs. As she pondered Psalm 1:2-3, which describes the faithful as "like a tree planted by streams of water," she realized that her Spirit-filled journey wasn't a single transformation but a steady, rooted growth.

One day, Annabelle found herself in a difficult conversation with a colleague. In the past, she might have become defensive or anxious, but something was different. She felt the Spirit nudging her to listen, to offer grace, and to respond gently. Her colleague later expressed appreciation for her patience, and Annabelle knew it was a moment shaped by her daily practice of surrendering to the Spirit.

The decision to cultivate a Spirit-filled lifestyle transformed Annabelle's perspective. Ordinary tasks, decisions, and interactions became sacred opportunities for connection with the Holy Spirit. She no longer felt overwhelmed by life's complexities; instead, she felt grounded and empowered. The simple act of inviting the Spirit into each day reshaped her relationships, refined her character, and infused her life with divine wisdom.

Annabelle's journey illustrates that a Spirit-filled lifestyle isn't about perfection but about presence—the presence of the Holy Spirit guiding and sustaining us each day. Her story reminds us that when we choose to walk in step with the Spirit, our lives become a canvas painted with His guidance, grace, and transformative power, turning the ordinary into the extraordinary.

Walking in Obedience to the Spirit

Obedience to the Holy Spirit is the linchpin of a Spirit-filled life. It's the conscious decision to align our will with the divine, to walk in step with the Spirit's gentle leading. Throughout Scripture, we encounter countless stories of individuals who heeded the Spirit's guidance, and their lives bore witness to the extraordinary impact of obedience.

Consider the story of Philip in Acts 8. The Spirit directed him to approach the chariot of an Ethiopian eunuch, leading to a profound encounter where the eunuch's life was forever changed through the proclamation of the gospel. Philip's obedience not only transformed the eunuch's life but also led to the spreading of the gospel to distant lands.

In our own lives, obedience to the Spirit's promptings can lead to remarkable outcomes. It may involve a simple act of kindness prompted by an inner nudge, leading to someone's day being brightened. It may entail a life-altering decision to pursue a specific calling or ministry, changing the course of our own journey and the lives of others. Obedience to the Spirit is not a burdensome task but an invitation to partake in divine adventures.

Yet, obedience isn't always easy. It often requires us to step out of our comfort zones, to confront fears and doubts, and to relinquish control. It's a journey of trust, knowing that the Spirit's guidance is rooted in love and wisdom. As we obey, we discover the abundant life Jesus promised in John 10:10, a life marked by fulfillment, purpose, and intimacy with God.

So, let us explore the transformative power of obedience to the Holy Spirit. Through stories of individuals who walked in obedience, we glimpse the beauty of a Spirit-filled life, where each step taken in faith becomes a testimony to God's faithfulness and guidance. In obedience, we find not only the path to a deeper relationship with God but also the privilege of participating in His divine purposes for our lives and the world around us.

In obedience, we experience a harmonious union between our will and God's divine plan. It's like a dance where the Spirit leads, and we follow, each step infused with purpose and grace. This partnership with the Holy Spirit doesn't stifle our individuality or creativity but amplifies them, as the Spirit empowers us to become all that God created us to be.

Obedience to the Spirit also equips us for the challenges of life. When faced with adversity, uncertainty, or temptation, we can rely on the Spirit's guidance to navigate through the storms. The apostle Paul, in Romans 8:14, assures us that "those who are led by the Spirit of God are sons of God." We become heirs to the promises of God, recipients of His wisdom and strength.

Yet, obedience is not a one-time decision but a daily choice. It's about waking up each morning with a heart attuned to the Spirit's whispers, seeking His guidance in the decisions we make, the words we speak, and the actions we take. As we yield to the Spirit's leading, we become vessels through which His love, joy, peace, patience, kindness, goodness, faithfulness, gentleness, and self-control flow into the world.

The rewards of obedience are profound. We witness the fruit of the Spirit growing in our lives, transforming our character and influencing our interactions with others. Our relationship with God deepens, and we find ourselves dwelling in the secret place of His presence, where intimacy and communion flourish. Obedience allows us to bear witness to the Spirit's transformative work not only within us but also through us, impacting the lives of those around us.

As we explore the concept of walking in obedience to the Spirit, we'll delve into stories that illuminate the challenges and triumphs of this journey. Through these narratives, we'll discover the remarkable ways in which obedience fosters spiritual growth, nurtures our relationship with God, and propels us into a Spirit-filled life where every moment becomes an opportunity to glorify Him.

The Power of Obedience to the Spirit

When Zacharias received a quiet nudge from the Holy Spirit to reach out to an old friend, he was unsure what it would lead to. It seemed like a simple prompt, but something in his heart told him it mattered. With a bit of nervousness, he picked up the phone and called. As the conversation unfolded, Zacharias learned that his friend had been struggling through a difficult season, feeling isolated and unsure where to turn. The friend's relief and gratitude for Zacharias's call were palpable; it was a lifeline in a time of deep need.

Reflecting on the experience, Zacharias was struck by how a simple act of obedience—one he might have brushed aside or ignored—could carry such profound significance. This wasn't a monumental or life-altering action, yet it had been exactly what his friend needed. Zacharias was reminded of Philip in Acts 8, who followed the Spirit's lead to speak with the Ethiopian eunuch. Philip's obedience had been the turning point for another's faith, just as Zacharias's phone call had brought his friend comfort and strength.

As Zacharias continued to practice listening to the Spirit, he noticed how obedience created a ripple effect, not just in others' lives but also in his own. Small, daily steps—whether a word of encouragement, an act of kindness, or a seemingly insignificant sacrifice—led to moments of grace and divine encounters. Each step became a testament to the faithfulness of God, who worked through Zacharias's obedience to reveal His love to those around him.

Zacharias's journey also brought him closer to God. The more he trusted and obeyed, the deeper his relationship with the Holy Spirit grew. He experienced what Jesus meant in John 10:10, discovering a life of purpose and joy beyond what he had imagined. Even in challenging moments, the Spirit's guidance was a source of peace and strength, reminding him that he didn't have to rely on his own understanding.

Through obedience, Zacharias realized he was part of something bigger—an adventure of faith that invited him to step beyond his comfort zone and trust in God's plan. His story reminds us that the Spirit's guidance often comes in whispers, urging us to follow with an open heart and a willingness to act, even when the full picture is unclear.

Zacharias's journey reflects the truth that obedience to the Spirit is a daily choice, an invitation to partner with God in small but meaningful ways. His experience shows us that a Spirit-filled life, rooted in obedience, transforms our ordinary moments into divine opportunities to reveal God's love and grace to the world.

Conclusion

As we conclude our exploration of living a Spirit-filled life, we find ourselves at the threshold of a profound truth: the Holy Spirit is not a distant or sporadic presence in our lives, but an ever-present guide, comforter, and source of power. Our journey through this chapter has illuminated the transformative impact of daily walking in the Spirit's embrace.

We've discovered that the Spirit doesn't reserve His guidance for special occasions but desires to be our constant companion in every moment. In the routine of our lives, we've encountered the extraordinary—a wisdom that surpasses human understanding, a love that knows no bounds, and a peace that defies circumstances.

We've learned that cultivating a Spirit-filled lifestyle is not about striving for perfection but about surrendering to the Spirit's leading, day by day and step by step. It's in this surrender that we find freedom, as the Spirit empowers us to overcome challenges, make choices aligned with God's heart, and experience the abundant life Jesus promised.

And as we've explored the concept of obedience to the Spirit, we've witnessed the beauty of a harmonious partnership, where our will aligns with God's divine plan. It's in this obedience that we discover not only the path to spiritual growth but also the privilege of participating in God's divine purposes for our lives and the world around us.

In living a Spirit-filled life, we become vessels through which the love, joy, peace, patience, kindness, goodness, faithfulness, gentleness, and self-control of the Spirit flow into the world. We become instruments of God's grace, agents of transformation, and bearers of His light.

As we close this chapter and this journey, may you carry with you the profound truth that the Holy Spirit is with you, not just in moments of extraordinary spiritual encounter, but in every moment of your ordinary, everyday life. Embrace the Spirit's guidance, yield to His leading, and experience the joy of daily walking in the unseen force of divine power. Your life will be forever transformed, and your impact on the world will be immeasurable.

Afterword

Where Do We Go from Here?

As we reach the conclusion of this transformative journey through "Spirit Filled Life: The Unseen Force of Divine Power," the third installment in The Living Waters Series, I want to extend my heartfelt gratitude to you. Your commitment to exploring the mysteries and revelations surrounding the Holy Spirit's work has been nothing short of inspiring.

Throughout this book, we've embarked on a profound expedition into the realms of faith, discovering the intimate relationship between believers and the Holy Spirit. We've witnessed how the Spirit's presence can infuse our lives with purpose, power, and transformation, transcending the boundaries of our understanding.

Yet, as we stand at the precipice of concluding this chapter, it is essential to recognize that our journey does not end here. In fact, it is merely the beginning of a lifelong exploration into the depths of the Spirit's work in our lives and the world around us.

Where Do We Go from Here?

Our journey doesn't end with the final page of this book; it merely marks the beginning of a new chapter in your own spiritual journey. So, where do we go from here?

1. **Embrace the Spirit**: Continue to cultivate your relationship with the Holy Spirit. Seek His guidance, His presence, and His empowerment in your daily life. Let His unseen force be the driving power behind your faith.

2. **Dive Deeper**: The Bible, as the Word of God, is a treasure trove of wisdom and revelation. In Book 4 of The Living Waters Series, "The Bible Unbound: Trust, Translation, and Transformation," we will explore the transformative power of Scripture. Dive into its pages, allowing it to deepen your understanding of God and His ways.

3. **Share the Journey**: Don't keep this journey to yourself. Share the insights and truths you've discovered with others. Encourage fellow believers on their path to a Spirit-

filled life and help them experience the divine power that lies within.

4. **Pray for Renewal**: Pray for a fresh outpouring of the Holy Spirit in your life, your community, and the world. Believe that His power can bring revival, transformation, and healing to all who call upon His name.

5. **Stay Connected**: Consider joining or forming a community of believers who share in the pursuit of a Spirit-filled life. Fellowship, accountability, and shared spiritual experiences can be incredibly enriching.

Reflect and Renew

Before we part ways, take a moment to reflect on the journey you've undertaken in this book. Consider the moments of revelation, the stories of transformation, and the whispers of the Spirit that have graced these pages. Allow the lessons learned to take root in your heart and mind.

Remember that the Spirit-filled life is not a destination but a lifelong pursuit. Embrace each day as an opportunity to draw nearer to God, to seek His will, and to be a vessel of His love and power.

As you close this book, envision your own path forward. Envision the ways in which you will continue to grow, to pray, and to walk in the guidance of the Holy Spirit. Envision the lives you will touch and the impact you will make as a Spirit-filled believer.

May the insights gained from this book be a source of inspiration and empowerment as you navigate the days and years ahead. The Spirit-filled life is a journey of infinite possibilities, and your story is still unfolding.

Thank you for allowing me to be a part of your journey. May your life be a testament to the unseen force of divine power, and may you walk boldly and faithfully in the guidance of the Holy Spirit.

With gratitude and hope,

Lori Ann Moeszinger

Bibliography

The Living Waters Series

In the quest to explore the depths of what it truly means to be a follower of Christ, the journey often leads us to the wisdom of many who have walked the path before us. "Passion for Christ: New Beginnings," along with its ten resulting volumes in The Living Waters Series, and then, "In sacred Conversation: The New Testament Prayer Guide" stands as a beacon, illuminating the various facets of Christian living.

The bibliography presented herein is not merely a list; it is a tapestry woven from the threads of countless believers, theologians, historians, and spiritual leaders whose insights and experiences have been invaluable in shaping the discourse within these pages. It serves as an atlas, guiding the earnest seeker through the landscapes of thought that have been traversed to bring these works to fruition.

Each book has been carefully selected to enrich understanding, to challenge preconceptions, and to offer solace and strength on this pilgrimage we embark upon in our daily lives. They are not just citations but conversations with the past, dialogues with the divine, and intersections with ideas that compel us towards a deeper, more profound faith.

As you peruse this bibliography, may it be more than a reference. May it become a repository of knowledge, a companion in study, and gateway to an ever-expanding world of theological richness and spiritual depth. Here lies the foundation upon which The Living Waters Series is built—each book contributing to the symphony of voices that call us to live out faith with vigor and sincerity.

May this bibliography serve you as your guide and inspiration, beckoning you to further exploration, deeper understanding, and a more passionate pursuit of the One who calls us to new beginnings.

The Living Waters Series

The Living Waters Series is a beacon for all those navigating the depths of Christian faith. Encompassing a collection of twelve transformative works, including the cornerstone overview, "Passion for Christ: New Beginnings," this series is a comprehensive journey through the core tenets of

Christianity. From the awakening of the soul to the embrace of eternity, each book delves into critical aspects of belief, practice, and divine experience. Readers are offered a wellspring of wisdom on salvation, baptism, filled with the Holy Spirit, Scripture, church community, tithing, giving, praying for unsaved loved ones, evangelism, and living a life that echoes beyond time. Crafted for both new believers and seasoned disciples, The Living Waters Series stands as a testament to the enduring power of faith and the relentless love of God that flows through every page.

Passion for Christ: New Beginning

Moeszinger, Lori Ann. Passion for Christ: New Beginnings. The Ridge Publishing Group, August 2024.

In her poignant and insightful book, "Passion for Christ: New Beginnings," Lori Ann Moeszinger embarks on an in-depth exploration of transformative Christian living, providing a vital resource for both new converts and long-standing believers seeking to renew their faith. As the first installment of The Living Waters Series, this volume not only introduces readers to the fundamental principles of living a Christ-centered life but also guides them through the practical aspects of incorporating these principles into daily activities and decisions.

Moeszinger adeptly combines theological depth with accessible writing to address the challenges of maintaining spiritual integrity in the modern world. With each chapter, she carefully unpacks the virtues of a life surrendered to Christ, using scriptural references and personal anecdotes to enhance the reader's understanding and application of biblical teachings. This book is an essential guide for anyone committed to pursuing a deep, authentic relationship with God through Jesus Christ, promising not just spiritual insights but a transformative journey of the heart and soul.

Faith On Trial:
The Startling Reality of Genuine Belief

Moeszinger, Lori Ann. Faith On Trial: The Startling Reality of Genuine Belief. The Living Waters Series. The Ridge Publishing Group, September 2024.

Lori Ann Moeszinger's "Faith On Trial: The Startling Reality of Genuine Belief" serves as the opening volume of The Living Waters Series, inviting readers into a compelling journey through the depths of authentic Christian faith. This book confronts essential questions about the nature of belief, the essence of grace, and the rigor of salvation with an unflinching clarity that is both challenging and enlightening.

Structured around critical examinations of foundational Christian doctrines—such as the Roman Road and the Four Spiritual Laws—"Faith On Trial" offers readers a rigorous pathway to assess and affirm the authenticity of their faith. Through thoughtful analysis and personal introspection,

Moeszinger encourages believers to scrutinize their spiritual convictions against biblical standards, providing a comprehensive guide to understanding and embracing a genuine Christian life.

Each chapter in "Faith On Trial" is designed not only to inform but to transform, urging readers to consider deeply the eternal implications of their faith and their readiness to stand before God. This book is a must-read for anyone seeking to deepen their spiritual understanding and to live out a faith that truly withstands the trials and tribulations of modern life.

Drenched in Faith:
The Transformative Act of Water Baptism

Moeszinger, Lori Ann. Drenched in Faith: The Transformative Act of Water Baptism. The Living Waters Series. The Ridge Publishing Group, October 2024.

In the second installment of The Living Waters Series, Lori Ann Moeszinger offers a profound exploration into the spiritual significance of baptism in "Drenched in Faith: The Transformative Act of Water Baptism." This book navigates through the historical, symbolic, and deeply personal aspects of baptism, presenting it as a crucial rite of passage for believers.

Moeszinger delves into the roots of baptism from its biblical origins to its modern-day applications, exploring how this ancient ritual acts as a bridge between personal faith and communal identity. The book provides a thorough investigation into whether baptism is merely a symbolic act or a necessary step towards salvation, examining its role in shaping Christian identity across the ages.

Each chapter of "Drenched in Faith" is designed to engage readers with theological insights and spiritual reflections, encouraging them to consider how baptism's transformative power can impact their own lives and the lives of those around them. From the cleansing waters of the Jordan River to the sacred spaces of contemporary churches, Moeszinger invites readers to rediscover baptism as a dynamic and ongoing act of faith that continues to resonate with profound spiritual significance.

This book is essential for anyone seeking to deepen their understanding of a foundational Christian practice. It challenges believers to rethink the role of baptism within the broader context of their spiritual journey, making it a vital resource for those looking to embrace a life truly drenched in faith.

Spirit Filled Life:
The Unseen Force of Divine Power

Moeszinger, Lori Ann. Spirit Filled Life: The Unseen Force of Divine Power. The Living Waters Series. The Ridge Publishing Group, November 2024.

BIBLIOGRAPHY

In the third installment of The Living Waters Series, Lori Ann Moeszinger takes readers on a profound journey into the supernatural realms of Christianity in "Spirit Filled Life: The Unseen Force of Divine Power." This book provides a comprehensive exploration of the Holy Spirit's dynamic role in the believer's life, from the dramatic events of Pentecost to the subtle guidances in daily living.

Moeszinger offers deep biblical insights, historical contexts, and personal testimonies to illustrate the transformative impact of being filled with the Holy Spirit. The book discusses various manifestations of the Holy Spirit, such as speaking in tongues and prophetic insights, and distinguishes between public expressions of faith and intimate spiritual experiences.

Each chapter is designed not only to inform but also to inspire and challenge readers to invite the Holy Spirit more fully into their lives. Moeszinger encourages a deeper engagement with the Spirit's power, promising readers a renewed sense of faith and a more profound understanding of God's presence.

"Spirit Filled Life" serves as both a theological guide and a practical manual for those seeking to enhance their spiritual journey through Holy Spirit empowerment. It is an essential resource for anyone wishing to explore the breadth and depth of the Spirit's work in their life and to experience the full potential of living a Spirit-empowered life.

The Bible Unbound:
Trust, Translation, and Transformation

Moeszinger, Lori Ann. The Bible Unbound: Trust, Translation, and Transformation. The Living Waters Series. The Ridge Publishing Group, December 2024.

In the fourth installment of The Living Waters Series, Lori Ann Moeszinger delivers a compelling exploration of the Bible in "The Bible Unbound: Trust, Translation, and Transformation." This book offers readers an in-depth look into the authenticity of Bible translations, the interpretation of prophecy, and the application of biblical truths to modern life.

Moeszinger expertly guides readers through the complex landscape of Scripture, addressing common misconceptions and highlighting the enduring relevance of the Bible. Through a blend of scholarly research and accessible writing, she explores how accurate translations impact our understanding of ancient texts and unpacks the most enigmatic prophecies with clarity.

Each chapter of "The Bible Unbound" serves as both a lesson in biblical scholarship and a testament to the transformative power of Scripture. Moeszinger encourages readers to delve deeper into their faith by engaging with the Bible in a way that is both informed and passionate. This book is an essential resource for anyone seeking to deepen their understanding of Scripture and its application to their daily lives, providing the tools needed to navigate the rich terrain of biblical teachings and to embrace the Bible's transformative power in personal and communal contexts.

"The Bible Unbound" is more than a guide; it is an invitation to experience the Bible as a living, breathing entity that offers renewal and guidance for believers seeking to align their lives with eternal truths. This work is an indispensable part of any Christian's library, offering profound insights that promise to enrich the reader's spiritual journey and understanding of their faith.

Prophets and Pulpits: Discerning Truth in the House of God

Moeszinger, Lori Ann. Prophets and Pulpits: Discerning Truth in the House of God. The Living Waters Series. The Ridge Publishing Group, January 2025.

In the fifth volume of The Living Waters Series, Lori Ann Moeszinger delivers a probing examination of modern church practices and prophetic claims in "Prophets and Pulpits: Discerning Truth in the House of God." This book challenges believers to cultivate a discerning spirit towards spiritual leadership and worship, encouraging a return to Scripture-based truth and authenticity.

Moeszinger navigates through the intricate landscape of contemporary Christian worship, offering a critical look at how cultural customs intersect with and often obscure biblical doctrines. The book addresses hot-button issues such as the validity of modern prophetic voices, the authenticity of church practices, and the origins of commonly accepted Christian holidays like Christmas, providing a balanced perspective rooted in solid theological research.

"Prophets and Pulpits" serves not only as an educational resource but also as a guide for personal and communal spiritual growth. Moeszinger equips readers with the tools necessary to discern genuine biblical teachings from prevalent myths, promoting a deeper understanding of what it means to engage in genuine worship and follow godly leadership.

The book is a vital resource for anyone seeking to deepen their knowledge of church doctrine and enhance their worship experience. It is particularly useful for those wishing to understand the nuances of prophetic claims and the dynamics of spiritual authority within the context of modern Christianity.

Through engaging narrative and rigorous analysis, "Prophets and Pulpits" offers a transformative look at the essentials of a robust Christian faith, making it an indispensable addition to any believer's library who is eager to ensure their faith practices are grounded in truth and aligned with the teachings of Scripture.

Beyond the Tithe:
The Transformative Power of Generous Faith

Moeszinger, Lori Ann. Beyond the Tithe: The Transformative Power of Generous Faith. The Living Waters Series. The Ridge Publishing Group, February 2025.

In the sixth installment of The Living Waters Series, Lori Ann Moeszinger takes readers on a profound journey in "Beyond the Tithe: The Transformative Power of Generous Faith," exploring the spiritual richness that emerges from transcending traditional tithing practices. This volume challenges and encourages readers to redefine their understanding of generosity and its profound impact on both the giver and the receiver.

Delving into the biblical foundations of giving and its implications for modern believers, Moeszinger expertly weaves together scriptural insights, personal stories, and theological reflections to illustrate how generosity extends far beyond monetary contributions. She explores the joy and spiritual growth that come from a life characterized by giving, urging readers to embrace a more expansive view of generosity as a core element of Christian faith.

"Beyond the Tithe" not only discusses the historical and biblical context of tithing but also encourages a deeper, more intentional practice of generosity. Through compelling narrative and actionable advice, Moeszinger inspires readers to integrate generosity into their daily lives as a means of fostering spiritual development and enriching their communities.

This book serves as an essential guide for anyone seeking to deepen their spiritual journey through the practice of generous living. It is an invaluable resource for understanding how the act of giving can transform lives, build lasting legacies, and reflect the love of Christ in tangible ways.

Join Lori Ann Moeszinger in discovering the transformative power of generosity and learn how expanding your practice of giving can lead to a richer, more fulfilling faith journey.

Heart of Abundance:
The Journey to Radical Giving and Receiving

Moeszinger, Lori Ann. Heart of Abundance: The Journey to Radical Giving and Receiving. The Living Waters Series. The Ridge Publishing Group, March 2025.

In the seventh book of The Living Waters Series, Lori Ann Moeszinger leads readers into the enriching world of generosity in "Heart of Abundance: The Journey to Radical Giving and Receiving." This volume delves into the transformative power of generosity, exploring how radical giving and receiving can fundamentally enrich one's life and spirit.

Moeszinger expertly combines compelling narratives with profound biblical insights, illustrating how the acts of giving and receiving are not just transactions but transformative experiences that reflect divine love and foster deep personal fulfillment. Through stories of individuals and communities engaging in acts of unprecedented generosity, the book inspires readers to open their hearts and extend their hands in ways that leave lasting impacts.

"Heart of Abundance" challenges its readers to rethink traditional perceptions of generosity and to embrace a lifestyle of abundant giving that aligns with biblical teachings. It encourages a holistic view of generosity that transcends mere material giving and receives, promoting a life enriched by spiritual depth and communal connection.

This book is an essential resource for anyone seeking to deepen their understanding of spiritual abundance and to practice generosity in transformative ways. It provides practical guidance and inspiring examples that equip readers to start their own journey of radical generosity, aiming to cultivate a legacy of love and purpose that resonates through their lives and beyond.

Join Lori Ann Moeszinger in "Heart of Abundance" to discover how embracing radical generosity can lead you to a life filled with joy, purpose, and abundant fulfillment.

Heaven's Reach:
Drawing the Unbelieving into the Fold

Moeszinger, Lori Ann. Heaven's Reach: Drawing the Unbelieving into the Fold. The Living Waters Series. The Ridge Publishing Group, April 2025.

In the eighth book of The Living Waters Series, Lori Ann Moeszinger tackles the profound power of intercessory prayer in "Heaven's Reach: Drawing the Unbelieving into the Fold." This volume delves into the spiritual practice of interceding for those who have not yet embraced faith, exploring the transformative impact such prayers can have on both the individual and the wider community.

Moeszinger expertly combines theological insights with practical advice, providing readers with a comprehensive guide to intercessory prayer. Through compelling stories and a deep biblical understanding, she illustrates how strategic and compassionate prayer can bridge the gap between skepticism and faith, transforming doubts into devotion and indifference into fervor.

"Heaven's Reach" is designed to empower readers to cultivate a deeper compassion for the unbelieving and to engage in the mission of evangelism through prayer. The book is a call to action, encouraging believers to take up the mantle of intercessors, fostering a legacy of faith that reaches beyond personal boundaries and into the hearts of those around them.

This installment is an essential resource for anyone looking to deepen their understanding of evangelistic prayer and its role in drawing the unbelieving into a life of faith. It offers not just knowledge, but also the tools needed for readers to become active participants in what Moeszinger describes as "the greatest commission given to mankind."

Join Lori Ann Moeszinger in "Heaven's Reach" to discover the profound joy and fulfillment that comes from engaging in the transformative power of prayer and witness the change it can bring to the world.

Breaking Silence:
The Charge to Uphold the Faith Out Loud

Moeszinger, Lori Ann. Breaking Silence: The Charge to Uphold the Faith Out Loud. The Living Waters Series. The Ridge Publishing Group, May 2025.

In the ninth book of The Living Waters Series, Lori Ann Moeszinger delivers a compelling call to action with "Breaking Silence: The Charge to Uphold the Faith Out Loud." This installment challenges believers to vocalize their faith boldly and effectively, transforming them from silent observers to vocal advocates for Christ in a world desperate for truth.

Through a blend of scriptural wisdom and actionable advice, Moeszinger equips readers to navigate the complexities of modern evangelism. She tackles the barriers that often keep Christians silent, offering strategies to overcome fear and resistance while encouraging a dynamic expression of faith that resonates in both personal interactions and broader societal engagement.

"Breaking Silence" serves as both a guide and an inspiration for Christians eager to make their faith audible in the cacophony of global discourse. It provides practical steps for engaging in vocal faith advocacy, emphasizing the importance of truth spoken with love and conviction. Moeszinger's insightful guidance helps readers harness the power of their voice to bridge gaps, heal divisions, and lead others toward the transformative power of the Gospel.

This book is an essential tool for anyone ready to take their faith expression to the next level, offering both the why and the how of effective communication. Prepare to be inspired, challenged, and equipped to make your faith heard in a world yearning for hope and direction.

Join Lori Ann Moeszinger in a movement that not only breaks the silence but also builds a legacy of faith that echoes through eternity.

Beyond the Final Breath: The Christian's Voyage into Eternity

Moeszinger, Lori Ann. Beyond the Final Breath: The Christian's Voyage into Eternity. The Living Waters Series. The Ridge Publishing Group, June 2025.

In the monumental finale of The Living Waters Series, Lori Ann Moeszinger provides readers with a profound exploration into the Christian perspective on life after death in "Beyond the Final Breath: The Christian's Voyage into Eternity." This book serves as a spiritual guide, offering deep biblical insights and thoughtful inquiries into the mysteries of the afterlife and the soul's journey beyond mortal existence.

Through a blend of scriptural interpretation and reflective exploration, Moeszinger challenges readers to consider the profound questions surrounding our eternal destiny. She navigates through complex theological terrain with clarity and compassion, addressing topics such as the nature of the eternal body, the significance of the Lamb's Book of Life, and what Scripture reveals about the afterlife.

"Beyond the Final Breath" is crafted not only to inform but also to inspire readers to align their earthly lives with God's eternal promises. It encourages a life that views its conclusion not as an end but as the commencement of a glorious, eternal existence. This book is an indispensable resource for anyone seeking to understand the biblical teachings on eternity and how they apply to personal faith and the broader Christian hope.

Join Lori Ann Moeszinger in this culminating volume as she guides you through the Christian eternal journey, preparing you for a life beyond death filled with hope and glory. This is more than just a book—it is a beacon for all who seek to live their earthly lives in anticipation of their eternal home.

In Sacred Conversation: Getting Your Prayer Life In Order

Moeszinger, Lori Ann. In Sacred Conversation: Getting Your Prayer Life In Order. The Living Waters Series Sequel. The Ridge Publishing Group, July 2025.

As a sequel to the widely acclaimed The Living Waters Series, Lori Ann Moeszinger's "In Sacred Conversation: Getting Your Prayer Life In Order" offers readers an insightful and practical guide to mastering the art of prayer according to New Testament principles. This book explores ten fundamental prayers, elucidating their significance and application in the daily lives of believers, aiming to deepen their communion with God.

The guide is meticulously structured to enhance the reader's understanding of effective prayer, incorporating scriptural foundations and practical steps to develop a disciplined prayer routine. Moeszinger integrates biblical insights with contemporary relevance, making each lesson accessible and actionable for modern Christians seeking to fortify their prayer lives.

"In Sacred Conversation" is designed not only to educate but also to transform, encouraging readers to integrate prayer seamlessly into their daily routine, thus enriching their spiritual journey and relationship with God. It serves as an essential resource for anyone eager to enhance their communication with the divine, providing the tools needed for a more profound, effective spiritual practice.

This sequel continues the tradition of The Living Waters Series by guiding readers through a detailed exploration of biblical teachings, encouraging them to live out their faith with confidence and sincerity. Ideal for both new and seasoned believers, "In Sacred Conversation" is more than just a book— it's a spiritual mentor for all who seek to align their prayer life with God's eternal promises.

ABOUT THE AUTHOR

Author Photo © 2023 Edwin Wolfe

LORI ANN MOESZINGER, affectionately known as "L," stands at the creative helm of The Ridge Publishing Group and its diverse imprints. A prolific American author, insightful blogger, and dynamic publisher, she crafts words that resonate and narratives that captivate. Now, nestled in the scenic tranquility of Coeur d'Alene, Idaho, Lori finds inspiration in the lakeside whispers and the companionship of her husband and their two beloved dogs.

Her writing journey traverses various pseudonyms, each a distinct facet of her expansive expertise. As Ann Patterson, she delves into the intricacies of business law, distilling complex concepts into clear, actionable advice. Under the byline L. A. Moeszinger, she navigates the nuanced realms of writing, marketing, and publishing, guiding aspiring authors toward their dreams. In her biblical and personal writings, she embraces her full name, Lori Ann Moeszinger, offering reflections steeped in faith and introspection.

Yet, it's through the New Youniversity Chronicles, The Manhattan Diaries series that Lori's versatility truly shines, showcasing her storytelling prowess across a spectrum of voices, each as engaging and unique as the last. Her foundational belief in faith's power, the virtue of blessings, and the virtues of industrious dedication pulses through every line she writes.

Transcending her former life as a lawyer, Lori now revels in the freedom of expression that authorship and publishing afford—a stark contrast to the rigid confines of law. Her new chapter is one marked by a fervent passion for empowering others, a commitment to hard work, and the joy of sharing her literary gifts.

Discover the multifaced worlds Lori has woven at her websites and blog sites, or connect with her on her social media platforms where she continues to inspire, educate, and transform the written word into a shared experience of growth and discovery.

Parent Website: https://www.RidgePublishingGroup.com and

blog site https://www.PublisherAndHerWorld.com

Publisher Website: https://www.GuardiansofBiblicalTruth.com and

blog site https://www.Jesus-Says.com

Author website: https://www.LAMoeszinger.com and New Youniversity sites:

https://www.NewYouniversity.com,
https://www.ManhattanChronicles.com

Bridge Website: https://www.AuthorsDoor.com and

blog site https://www.AuthorsRedDoor.com

Entertainment website: https://www.EthanFoxBooks.com and

blog site https://www.KidsStagram.com

Want More?

Welcome to Coffee with God! Jesus-Says.com! Dive into our blog for inspiring insights and biblical truths that deepen your faith and enrich your spiritual journey. Explore thought-provoking articles, personal testimonies, and practical guidance rooted in Scripture. Whether you're new to the faith or a lifelong believer, Jesus-Says offers wisdom and encouragement for your walk with Christ. Join our community and grow in your relationship with God!

Guardians of Biblical Truth Hub

Welcome to our Guardians of Biblical Truth Facebook page! Join our community to deepen your understanding of the Bible and live out its principles. Engage in enriching Bible studies, share faith testimonies, and connect with like-minded believers. Whether you're new to the faith or a seasoned believer, you'll find support and inspiration here. Join us today and grow in your walk with Christ.

Guardians of Biblical Truth Forum

Welcome to our Guardians of Biblical Truth Forum! Join our closed Facebook group to deepen your understanding of the Bible and strengthen your faith. Engage in enriching discussions, share personal testimonies, and connect with a supportive community of believers. Whether you're new to the faith or a seasoned believer, you'll find inspiration and encouragement here. Join us today and grow in your walk with Christ!